PETER
BRUEGEL

1. THE PAINTER AND THE CONNOISSEUR *(after 1565) Ink drawing, 25 × 21.6 cm (reproduced in original dimensions).*

BRUEGEL

by

Michael Gibson

Translated from the French and
Revised by the Author

THE WELLFLEET PRESS
WELLFLEET

2. CHRIST IN LIMBO *Detail.*

To my children

Emmanuel
Marguerite
Matthew
Olivia

*That their world
may emerge from
the cave of unmeaning.*

Published by
WELLFLEET PRESS
110 Enterprise Avenue
Secaucus, New Jersey 07094

ISBN: 1-55521-473-8

Printed and bound in Hong Kong.

Contents

The Tenor of the Times

*Every essence, every idea, belongs to a specific realm of history and geography.
This does not imply that they are locked into this realm and inaccessible to
others. Only one can no more hope to get a quick overview of the time and space
of culture, than one can get one of those of nature. Communication between
one established culture and another can only be achieved by passing through
that wild region in which both of them were born.*

Maurice Merleau-Ponty

Of all the painters of past centuries, Peter Bruegel can, at times, strike one as the most familiar and accessible. Though it lies four hundred years in the past, his world is much like our own. We encounter our seasons in his landscapes; we can drift into them, as though making our way home in the footsteps of the bone-weary hunters he depicts, of the ox herds he shows hastening before the storm. The house hunched down in the hollow is one we have lived in; the bonfire, with its strong, windblown flame must once have warmed our hands. And, that old woman, bent double beneath her load of kindling on the snowy bridge, have we not often listened to the drone of her voice, smiled at her jibes, savored her cakes, and breathed her unwashed smell?

All this can appear quite familiar, but then we come upon other, entirely different works—*The Seven Deadly Sins* and *The Virtues*, *The Triumph of Death*, *The Battle of Carnival and Lent*, or *Crazy Griet (Dulle Griet)*. These all take us into a totally unfamiliar world. We may be able to sense its mood at times, but the topical speech of everyday life to which these pictures refer has become utterly foreign to us today. The dreams they seem to echo are quite unlike any of our own, and if we wish to interpret them, we shall have to turn to a dream book of the kind that the historian's careful work can, up to a point, provide. For Bruegel and his age can, at times, appear very close to our own in outlook and sensibility, and quite alien to it at others. It is in fact this dual aspect of the work that can make it so attractive to us. For we can look down upon his period, with a backward glance over the bannister, as we go spinning off in the dizzy upward spiral of history. We can, up to a point, recognize

some characteristic features and attitudes of our own times, but we can also feel attracted by its entirely exotic spice, its distant charm.

The points both periods have in common may also allow us to understand Bruegel's work rather better today than it has been in the past, to delight in it for more appropriate reasons. Above all we now sense a seriousness in it that was ignored in former times by those who assumed that Bruegel was merely a gifted painter of grotesque subjects, at best delightfully picturesque, at worst deplorably trivial. His period was, like our own, a time of transition within the broader sweep of history—and this transition left a strong imprint on people's representations of the world. Bruegel's society had to face the consequences of the collapse of the feudal order—a collapse which had begun to affect not only the way people saw the world but even the way they conceived the import of their lives. The dissolution of this entrenched economic system affected the entire range of human relations. Widespread change caused perceptible dismay to people of every social class. All this appears quite obvious to us in retrospect. Time provides the necessary detachment. Yet those who live through a period of transition can hardly know the cause of their discomfort, nor guess which way the drift will carry them. They may experience a peculiar dizziness, or again they may get used to the creeping malaise of the times, just as a person may adjust to the slow progression of a disease.

The sixteenth century, then, was the end of something, but it was also a dawning—the dawning of the northern Renaissance, which led to the consolidation of the bourgeois (i.e., urban) financial order and to the relative eclipse of the old, landowning nobility. It is no doubt easier to sense an ending than to perceive the beginning of something as yet unknown. The decaying feudal system had had real benefits as well as obvious flaws; at the very least, it had provided a familiar order of daily life and livelihood, of laws and customs, so that change was not entirely welcome. In those days, just as in our own, new inventions often bred unemployment. New weaving machines, new techniques for dyeing wool, introduced into the Netherlands by the merchant economy (which had, by now, become the long-term master of history), provoked riots among workers. Some of these machines, in fact, were temporarily banned by magistrates who deplored their disruptive impact on employment. For better or for worse, these same objective factors led to the consolidation of great nation states: Charles V imposed his central power on Austria and Spain; François I did as much in France; Henry VIII, in England. These new political structures might well remind one of the tremendous towers of Babel painted by Bruegel, with the monarch standing in the foreground. The exactions of the Duke of Alva in the Netherlands must be regarded as no more than a minor episode unfolding in the shadow of these greater undertakings.

All these innovations went hand in hand with new ways of thinking. The world was no longer perceived in predominantly magical, supernatural, or symbolic terms. Nor were relationships as exclusively personal as they once had been. Instead the world was beginning to be viewed from an objective and practical point of view, and all things were being examined anew in the then unfamiliar terms of cause and effect. It appeared increasingly obvious and acceptable that events were not being directly shaped by the will of God or by the intervention of his saints, but rather were the consequences of that body of observable, unchanging laws that we generally have in mind when we speak of Nature.

Galileo, to be sure, would not appear on the scene until the seventeenth century. Only then would the experimental method of science be clearly outlined for the first time—but the new sap had begun to rise some centuries earlier, however timidly. Popular legend had even regarded the entirely orthodox theologian Albertus Magnus (1193–1280) as something of a warlock or a magus, because he happened to take an interest in certain natural sciences and had ventured to make some observations of his own. According to legend, he kept in his study a bronze head that could answer all questions touching on natural causes. This legend, though still saturated with magical dread, strikes us as a peculiar anticipation of the potentials of present-day technology. Or is it that we ourselves still invest technology with a magical aura?

In the medieval view all questions touching upon cause were ordered according to a strict hierarchy: The true and founding cause, the only one that really mattered, was God's will, aided or hampered by the lesser wills of men. So it could appear both pointless and ungodly to inquire after material causes without first inquiring into the will of God. Yet the new merchant society, whose power and outlook was now gaining the upper hand, tended to view such matters in a different light. Merchandise has no latent magic to it. It has stable, or at least predictable, characteristics, and if wheat happens to rot in transit, there is no need to look beyond natural causes. Who indeed could be better motivated than a merchant to find out whether the earth actually *was* round as some people suggested—for the answer could mean a shorter route to the Indies, swifter transportation of spices and of silk, and a quicker profit. The new outlook on the world was thus the result of a transition from the primacy of a land-based political power and economy to the primacy of trade and industry. With these came a practical attitude that tended to take only straightforward material causes into account. Such an outlook was quite new in its day; its strangeness and apparent inhumanity frightened many people.

It is hardly surprising, then, that this age of enlightenment should also have seen the very first appearance of an *official* belief in witchcraft and in a diabolical plot aimed at the domination of this nether world—a putsch or coup engineered by the powers of Hell. All this was no more than the transposition, in the shape of a perverse *personal* will or intention, of the entirely *impersonal* (and consequently still largely inconceivable) power of material cause. The witch craze, then, and its thousands of stakes may be regarded as the grim shadow cast by the pure light of the Renaissance, an expression of the anxiety its sheer novelty provoked.

But, one may ask, was not this shadow merely a survival of the medieval night? Not at all! It was, on the contrary, a new parasitic growth, and its advances more or less coincided with that of the development of inquiries in the field of natural sciences—the sort of inquiries first undertaken by Albertus Magnus among others. The common folk, of course, had always believed in witches; who else could cause cows to die or crops to rot? These shifty-eyed figures with their pernicious gaze were well known to all and sundry throughout the county. Yet the Church, over the centuries, had stubbornly refused to admit things that popular belief considered obvious, and on this point the temporal powers had supported it. In recently converted Saxony, Charlemagne even imposed the death penalty on those who ventured to burn a presumed witch. According to H. R. Trevor-Roper, he decreed it to be "a heathen custom."[1]

The official doctrine of the Church touching upon these matters had not varied throughout the Middle Ages. Things first began to change in the twelfth century—under the influence of the Inquisition.[2] But it was only in 1485, on the threshold of the sixteenth century, that

[1] These facts and figures are drawn from H. R. Trevor-Roper, *The European Witch Craze of the XVIth and XVIIth Centuries.* I cannot venture to present the substance of Trevor-Roper's thesis here, but it is basic to any understanding of the period and does not, I hope, preclude the line of reasoning I have adopted here.

[2] According to Trevor-Roper, demonology was an inverted theology entirely elaborated by the Dominican inquisitors. They were not aware of this, of course, but it was the predictable consequence of leading questions put to people under torture.

this organization finally won a complete reversal of the doctrine that the Church had explicitly defended until then.[3] With this reversal it also obtained permission to use various unsavory means to root out witchcraft in Germany. Only then did it become permissible to torture and burn persons accused of practicing witchcraft. And, in the grim power struggle then under way, this permission would prove useful both to the Reformation and to the Counter-Reformation.

The Devil is a familiar figure in medieval art—that cannot be denied. He often shows his face in the New Testament too. Thomas Aquinas, in the broad context of his *Summa Theologica*, came up with some rather unexpected notions of preternatural biology in his discussion of the behavior of incubi and succubi—the male and female demons who were thought to cause obsessive erotic fantasies and sleepless nights and, occasionally, to beget creatures half human, half devil. (*Rosemary's Baby* is a modern transposition of this sort of anxiety.)

According to the Angelic Doctor, the Devil had no generative powers of his own. An incubus could only impregnate a woman by discharging what he had first absorbed as a succubus. "He therefore nimbly alternated," Trevor-Roper concludes, "between these postures. . . ." (p. 18) The remarkable thing is that the officially sanctioned belief in a devilish plot, aimed at taking over the earth before the divinely ordained term of human history had been reached, spread through Europe in the fullness of its power only in the sixteenth century. The attending reign of terror extended over two centuries. Johann Wolfgang von Goethe had already written the first draft of *Faust* when the last legal witch burning was carried out in Switzerland in 1782. This new craze tends to explain why devils, with their legions of witches and warlocks, should have quite suddenly turned up in the art and literature of the beginning of the sixteenth century—in the paintings of Heironymus Bosch and Peter Bruegel, to be sure, but also in the writings of William Shakespeare (in *Macbeth*, for instance) and later in those of John Milton (in *Paradise Lost*). This kind of material does not appear in the same perspective in earlier literature—except in specialized works.

Witchcraft, once a totally unsystematic body of rural beliefs, acquired a new meaning in these changing times: The terrifying Devil of objectivity with his impersonal power had launched himself upon the conquest of the world. Something was indeed rotten here below—the times, as Shakespeare would soon observe, were out of joint. The best remedy to this, some supposed, was to burn several thousand men, women, and children, rich and poor, noble and commoner, at the stake. A few enlightened minds did attempt to argue against such beliefs. One of them was Johann Weyer, a humanist and a doctor with a practice in Holland. The only result he achieved was to have his book put on the Index of Forbidden Books by the governor of the Netherlands, the Duke

of Alva, who further obtained the doctor's dismissal from the court of Cleves. The witch-hunt was also fanned by the religious wars. The pacification of Flanders by Catholic Spain led to the burning of a large number of unfortunate people whose orthodoxy was found wanting. Had not the king of Spain himself decreed in his letters patent that witchcraft was the scourge and destruction of the human race? While a nightmare for the people, it was also a handy political tool for those in power—though its explosive force naturally called for utmost care in handling.

Bruegel's world was not that of the Renaissance, even though its wide perspectives appear to welcome it. His youth had been deeply rooted in the medieval. The northern countries have none of the vestiges of antiquity familiar in the south, nothing like the colossal monuments that could be found gradually crumbling away at the very center of the big cities—the Baths of Caracalla, for instance, or the Coliseum—or even in the countryside, the once thriving villas and the tombs. Rural Germany in the medieval period was still largely covered with boundless forests, their silence, their murmurings, their perils. This atmosphere still colors the tales recorded some centuries later by the brothers Grimm. The Netherlands in those days still had great stretches of unpopulated land, though one may find this hard to believe as one visits that crowded country today. Except for the stones raised by the Celts, the northern gods had left no vestiges behind them. So the only monuments found in the cities of the north were those of the Christian era. This may help account for the fact that, despite the pervasiveness of the Italian influence and its tremendous prestige, a Gothic tone persisted in the customs and architecture of the north up to the twentieth century. J. Huizinga's *Waning of the Middle Ages* offers some penetrating insights into the spiritual and social soil that nurtured Bruegel's work. What situations and events marked the daily lives of people in those days? What did their imaginations feed on? On the ritual of holy days, says Huizinga, on processions, both sacred and profane; on solemnized events of everyday life—the rites and customs surrounding births, weddings, and deaths; on executions, long-drawn-out torture and ferocious punishment on the public square; on carnivals and street dances (which sometimes attained the highest pitch of hysteria); on public sermons, too, that whipped up a frenzy of emotions such as can hardly be imagined today.

"The modern reader of newspapers," says Huizinga, "can no longer conceive the violence of impression caused by the spoken word on an ignorant mind lacking mental food." The Franciscan Friar Richard preached in Paris in 1429 during six consecutive days. He began at five in the morning and spoke without a break till ten or eleven, for the most part in the cemetery of the Innocents ("on whose walls," the French version of Huizinga's book adds, "was painted the famous danse macabre" and standing before the ossuary "in which skulls were piled up in full view"). When at the close of the tenth sermon, he announced that it would be his last, since he had no license to preach more, great and small wept as touchingly and bitterly as

[3] The bull "Summis desiderant affectibus" (1484) of Pope Innocent VII, who, in all other respects, was an enlightened humanist of the Renaissance.

Triumph of Death (15th
century Dutch)

if they were watching their best friends being buried; and
so did he. Thinking that he would preach once more at
Saint Denis on the Sunday, the people flocked thither
on Saturday evening and spent the night in the open to
secure good seats." When the famous Dominican preacher
Vincent Ferrer spoke, "his pulpit had to be protected by
a fence against the pressure of the congregation that
wanted to kiss his hands or habit. He rarely failed to
move his auditors to tears. When he spoke of the Last
Judgment, of Hell or the Passion, both he and his hearers
wept so copiously that he had to suspend his sermon till
the sobbing had ceased. Malefactors threw themselves
at his feet, before every one, confessing their great sins."

As Huizinga points out, emotions were more direct
and violent in an age marked by great ordeals and uncertainties, an age whose form of rationality was still quite
remote from our own. He has the fifteenth century in
mind, to be sure, but as we shall see, some of its characteristic features persisted well into the sixteenth. Cruelty
too, was straightforward and untempered. Daily life displayed tremendous contrasts in full view. Destitution
and wealth walked side by side, rotting lepers marched
about processionally, and misshapen beggars provoked
revulsion and pity on the steps of churches. The constant
and obvious fickleness of fortune might, under such circumstances, be regarded as a consolation of sorts, and
people could at the same time feel pity and derive some
measure of comfort at the sight of a once powerful man
being led to the gallows not, as one might expect, with
his head shorn and in a shirt, but, in order to provide a
good show, dressed up in his finest clothes and wearing
his golden spurs. And the headless corpse was later hung
from the gallows still wearing these clothes, and with his
spurs still at his heels (Huizinga).

And what about music? What sort of music could be
heard in those days? Giovanni Palestrina and Orlando
Lassus were both close contemporaries of Bruegel's. Claudio
Monteverdi was born only two years before the painter's
death. The almost unlimited realm of music that is our
daily fare today could not even have been anticipated in
people's remotest dreams. What music there was might
well strike us as repetitive and obsessional today (like
rock music now, and quite as wild, though with a less
brutal tone), slicing its unending furrow in the mind
through rowdy carnival nights and frequent street festivities. Court music, on the other hand, was something
quite different. The lute was one of the instruments then
in favor, and airs were sung that, though subtle and full

of delicate craft, may somehow fail to stir us. Church
music was both scholarly and polyphonic, still devoid of
the flourish and drama that was to come only later, a
richly woven arras, a precious, functional object created
for use in the ritual domain.

But yet another sound, says Huizinga, set its mark on
the hours, the days, and the seasons: the ubiquitous
clamor of the bells. Walking through the streets of Bruges
or some other northern city today, one may still get an
inkling of what it must have been like then. The hours
are told, even today, by the chimes in the high belfry
and, one by one, the church bells in various parts of the
city seem to pick up the tune. But all this is no more
than a distant echo of the role played by the bells when
they were the main harbingers of good and bad tidings.
Joy made them peal and riot; mourning sent dark tolling
notes scudding over the rooftops till they dropped like
pebbles into the dark waters of the canals. Danger sometimes roused the great, grim bell of the tocsin. The
French language, in the word *effroi* (derived from the latin
Exfredus), still echoes the impression it could make.
Exfredus signifies the breaking of the peace; to ring the
tocsin was termed in French *sonner l'effroi*; and terror
(*effroi* in French, even today) was presumably the chief
emotion felt by those who heard this bell. In fact, the
tocsin bell of the city of Antwerp, where Bruegel began
his career, was christened *Orida* (horrible) when it was
cast in 1316 (Huizinga). The election of a pope, the birth
of a prince, some bright and cheerful news would set
whole cities to clanging and tinkling from dawn to sun-
down. People had no other source of information, nor
could one imagine a better form of publicity in those
days than the ringing of the city's bells.

At the date we suppose Bruegel to have been born
(1525), the earth had only been deemed round for some
thirty years (1492, Christopher Columbus in America).
But it had still not begun spinning around the sun, and
Nicolaus Copernicus' *De Revolutionibus Orbium Coeles-
tium*, published in 1542, was received with widespread
indifference. Bruegel was presumably seventeen years old
at the time. The astronomer prudently offered his revolu-
tionary notions as though they were no more than a
hypothesis. Bruegel must have heard about them, some
ten years later, through his good friend the geographer
Abraham Ortels (Ortelius) of Antwerp. Only then, and
quite gradually, did this planet, which had seemed the
very foundation of the universe, begin to loose its moor-
ings and take off like a rudderless barge, adrift among the
stars.

At the same time cracks had begun to appear in the
monolith of Christendom—and they would ultimately
split it wide open. Martin Luther founded his church
when Bruegel, as we suppose, was just one year old (1526).
The following year the troops of Emperor Charles V
sacked pontifical Rome. The two powers, which since
the time of Charlemagne had regarded themselves as
complementary, were going through one of their regular
crises. When Bruegel reached adulthood, he witnessed
violent religious uprisings and persecutions in the Netherlands. In 1550 Charles V, who also ruled these lands,

published his "placards" (or edicts) in Flanders, declaring heretics to be seditious persons and disturbers of the common peace. They must all be put to death—the men, he decreed, should die by the sword, while the women should be buried alive.

In the 1560s, during the reign of Charles' gloomy son, Philip II, repression became increasingly severe: Anyone caught buying, selling, or reading a heretical book, anyone who dared beg a reprieve for a heretic (even for a father or a son) would be condemned to death. This failed to dampen the zeal of the reformed preachers who organized clandestine meetings in the woods. In August 1566 Calvinist preachings against the Catholic idols provoked violence against images in churches. The disturbances grew, and in three weeks, four hundred churches lay devastated. Documents have preserved, as if in amber, the image of a man who was caught, judged, and executed for the part he took in such deeds: Ghyslebrecht Cools, a thirty-five-year-old plumber, went to the scaffold in wide-eyed astonishment: "He had been roused from his bed at night to come help break the statues," a chronicler of the period reports. "He had not realized that this was a misdeed, and he very much deplored that he should have to die, considering that he was innocent."

The following year the Duke of Alva and his mercenaries reached Belgium. They had only recently fought the Moslems, and in their sight, heretics were no better. Eight thousand people perished during the years of Alva's pacification. Heretics who had been judged and sentenced were required to make their peace with the Church before dying—so the duke decreed. Should they refuse to die in the Catholic faith, he added, "let the tip of their tongue be burned with a hot iron before they leave prison for the place of execution."

When Bruegel was only ten years old, long before these events, the northern countries had been stunned by the Armaggedon of the Anabaptists (1535). This shocking incident must have impressed public opinion in much the same way that the massacre and mass suicides of Jonestown in Guyana impressed people a few years ago. However, the Anabaptist adventure involved a far larger number of people and left some 30,000 dead. The Anabaptist doctrines looked attractive to the dispossessed, to workers reduced to unemployment by new industrial methods, to beggars and marginal persons of every kind, to confused and visionary minds who responded in their own way to strange new circumstances. Marguerite Yourcenar, in *L'Oeuvre au noir*, also portrays wealthy, charitable persons embarking upon the wild adventure that ended in the bloodbath of Münster.

The egalitarian Anabaptists, in thought and words at least, stripped burghers of their wealth, nobles of their titles and position. Antwerp banished the Anabaptists in 1534, but they found an unexpected asylum in the city of Münster. The burghermaster welcomed them cordially, and they settled there in strength after running the bishop out of town. It all began, as in our own days, with generous evangelical notions of brotherly sharing and of perfect equality, and with the expectation that the arrival of God's kingdom on earth was imminent. But the bishop the Anabaptists had evicted gathered an army and returned to besiege his own town. After the death of Jan Matthys, the first leader of the Anabaptists, Hans Bockhold ("a wandering mountebank," says Yourcenar), was proclaimed prophet-king. He was thereafter referred to as John of Leyden. The siege drew out. Within the walls, the merely lukewarm were put to death. Blasphemers and fornicators were regularly hung. Bockhold, taking advantage of the feverish state of mind of a population under siege, assumed the prerogatives of an absolute leader. A once evangelical equality gradually made way for something utterly different. The terrified burghers offered him their women, and he graciously welcomed them. In the end he had acquired eighteen wives in this manner, and nobody dared suggest that he should hang.

The Anabaptists hoped for the end of the world which would prove them right. Instead they saw a Protestant army march up to give the Catholic bishop an unexpected helping hand. The town was delivered up by treachery; a massacre followed. "Throughout the day," writes Marguerite Yourcenar, "the heavy footsteps of soldiers rang through the city; their rhythmic beat declared that common sense had regained its rights in the citadel of the mad—the place was now under the control of men who sold their lives for a specific wage, drank and ate at regular hours, plundered and raped on occasion, but who had an old mother or a thrifty wife somewhere, and a small farm to which they would return, old and crippled, to live out their lives; men who went to mass when they were forced to and who believed in God with moderation. Once more there was torture, but this time it was decreed by the legitimate authority, approved by both the Pope and Luther. In the sight of the well-fed mercenaries, these gaunt and ragged people, their gums rotting away from the effects of famine, were merely a revolting vermin which it seemed both easy and fitting to destroy." (*L'Oeuvre au noir*). Thirty thousand people perished in the ensuing carnage.

A similar adventure, as I have already suggested, unfolded not long ago in Guyana. When the old order collapses, the poor (who are the first to feel the pangs of hunger), the confused and addled hearts and minds of those who perceive more keenly than others do the anxieties of a vacillating age, may sometimes allow themselves be carried away by strange hopes. The prophet may be even more stricken than the people who follow him. It is in such events, the mark of all uncertain times, that Bruegel's day and our own stand like brothers, hand in hand.

The disorders that afflicted the Netherlands in the years of Bruegel's maturity had a twofold origin. On the one hand there was the fiscal pressure resulting from the poor administration of the Spanish empire and the unreasonable demands of Philip II (who had taken upon himself the impossible task of running his enormous empire from Madrid—and handling everything, down to the minutest details, himself). Strange to say, the gold of Mexico and of Peru rarely found its way into the royal coffers. Also the tax laws of Spain granted exemptions to the very people who owned the greatest amount of taxable goods:

the nobility and the clergy. Much of the state revenue was raised through a ten percent value-added tax, unheard of in other parts of Europe, which kept Spanish trade from being competitive. As a result of all this the Spanish treasury had become far too dependent on taxes paid in by merchants of the big trading centers of the Netherlands: Antwerp and Amsterdam. So much for the first cause. As for the second, Philip II was much concerned by the inroads made by Protestantism precisely in these northern parts: Nobles and burghers of the opposition leaned towards Luther; workers, craftsmen and peasants were more inclined to attend the Calvinists. In Spain, from the very outset, the Inquisition had been so implacably repressive that the Reformation had never managed to take root. Philip II believed that a firm hand in the Netherlands would have the same effect.

He had entrusted the government of these remote provinces to his half-sister, Margaret, Duchess of Parma, the daughter of a Flemish mistress of Charles V. She was assisted by three advisers, the chief of these being Cardinal Antoine Perrenot de Granvelle (who, incidentally, is believed to have owned some paintings by Bruegel). Margaret was not disliked, and she might have governed easily enough had she not been obliged to enforce the fiscal and religious policies commanded by her brother's secret instructions. The presence of Spanish troops irritated the population. The nobility and the influential bourgeoisie resented the fact that they were given no share in government.

Three members of the nobility tried to obtain the dismissal of Cardinal Granvelle, whom they held responsible for these hateful policies. They were the Counts Lamoral d'Egmont and Philip de Hornes and Prince William of Orange. In response to their pressure, Granvelle was finally ousted. Egmont then went to Spain to submit a list of grievances to the king in person. Predictably enough, his embassy accomplished nothing. Faced with this failure and fearing that the Inquisition might soon be established in their country with its attending social and economic disorders, a wider alliance of young noblemen went to the governor and begged her to revoke the "placards." "You have nothing to fear, Madame," one of her advisers reportedly said, "They are nothing but beggars (*ce ne sont que des gueux*)." They were indeed begging a royal favor, but the word struck home, and in due course the anti-Spanish resistance would use it as a banner. Rebellion was brewing, even though Egmont, de Hornes, and William of Orange did their best to contain it. It was at this point (in 1566), that the outbreak of iconoclasm occurred—Bruegel was then about forty-one.

King Philip promptly reacted by sending the Duke of Alva to the Netherlands, with instructions to crush the rebellion even at the cost of "the total destruction of the country." He was also to arrest Egmont, de Hornes, and William of Orange and have them executed. Orange fled to Germany. Egmont and de Hornes were caught and beheaded on the main square of Brussels in June 1568. In the crowd stood a young man no one had yet heard of: Miguel de Cervantes. From the Spanish point of view, the execution was a political blunder, and in time the Spanish king would have to bear the consequences. Actions initiated by William of Orange ultimately led to the creation of the United Provinces. Flanders bled. Eight thousand people were put to death without the benefit of trial. In order to pay his troops, Alva had to levy taxes on the spot, and he did so by imposing the ten percent value-added tax that had, until then, been unknown in the Netherlands and that had already had such a harmful effect on the Spanish economy. Businessmen, who might not have been all that sensitive to other considerations, were touched to the quick. Their patriotism was aroused. The population was thus united when rebellion broke out in 1569 (Bruegel died that year, at the age of forty-four). Alva obstinately pursued his policy for six years. Then, realizing the situation had turned into a deadlock, he asked to be recalled. His mercenaries, however, remained on the spot—a constant danger to the local population. In 1576, having received no pay for two years, they decided to help themselves. The wealthy city of Antwerp was taken and plundered, and seven thousand of its citizens were slaughtered.

Such, in broad outline, were the events that left their mark on Bruegel's country during his lifetime. His works were steeped in this mood of crisis, even if they do not explicitly refer to it. So they can, in the broadest sense, be said to bear its imprint.

Bruegel's Life

One would like to be able to present a clear picture of Bruegel's life, of the opinions he held, and of the stand he took in the face of the political, religious, and philosophical upheavals that marked his period and the region in which he lived.

But the closer we try to get to the man, the more his profile seems to fade, and one may be reminded of the young photographer, in Antonioni's *Blow-Up* who, as he enlarges his photograph, gradually sees the presumed murderer and his gun fade into a shapeless cloud of silver nitrate crystals. A whole variety of conjectures concerning Bruegel arise to tempt us. The hypotheses are attractive, but authentic documents that actually provide positive information are rare.

A person close to me happened to be visiting Bruges in the 1930s. At one point, pausing to rest, he leaned against the parapet of a canal and admired the view—the stepped gables, the brick towers of the Belfry and of the Church of the Savior, the hog-backed bridges, the dark and silent water. After a moment an old man tottered up, leaned against the parapet beside him and spat reflectively into the water. "Beautiful, isn't it?" he asked.

The visitor agreed. It was indeed beautiful.

The old man shook his head knowingly: "It was much more beautiful *before . . .*"

"Before what?" the visitor inquired. He was sure that World War I had not touched the city

"Before the Spaniards came," the old man replied, spitting the word out like a bitter mouthful.

I was reminded of this story as I read the recent accounts of Bruegel's life in books by Belgian authors that, in other respects, offer a wealth of scrupulously researched facts. One can sense that the anger and revolt, bred by two more recent periods of occupation, has been projected onto the events that occurred in the sixteenth century, and onto their brutal climax, which lasted over a decade. These authors sometimes appear to wish that Bruegel, standing on that distant crest of time where we can barely make him out, had shared the feelings of the present day, that he should, in his own time, have cut the figure of a *"résistant."* They consequently leap at every clue that might suggest that this or that painting was, in fact, a pamphlet against the Spanish occupation and a satire against intolerance.

Karel van Mander, chronicler of Flemish painters (and a painter himself), does indeed relate that Bruegel, on his deathbed, told his wife to burn a number of drawings with inscriptions that he considered too mordant or satirical. Either he felt remorse, says van Mander, or he feared that they might get his wife into trouble. Van Mander most likely heard about the matter from Bruegel's second son, Jan, who must have learned it from his mother—his father died when Jan was only one year old. Bruegel did indeed turn out some satirical works—there is no cause to doubt van Mander's assertion on this point—but these are precisely the works (on what subjects? we don't know) that were destroyed. If satirical references are to be found in the surviving works, they must have been thoroughly camouflaged to avoid the risks of censorship or worse, and it would seem rather presumptuous to assume that we can detect them today. Consider the example of Johann Nestroy, the nineteenth-century Austrian theater and cabaret humorist who was once sent to jail for a couple of days for having ventured some ironical remarks about the high prices of bread. When he was released, he returned to the stage as though nothing had happened. He made no reference to the price of bread, but he wore buttons in the shape of breadrolls on his costume, and his wordless entrance, the seemingly negligent gesture with which he stroked the buttons, were perfectly understood by all and provoked the audience to knowing laughter. The fact is known today only because someone recorded it in writing—and the censors must have been aware of it too, but they could hardly make an issue of it without exposing themselves to ridicule. A picture of Nestroy wearing buttons shaped like breadrolls would be quite meaningless to us, unless some other source of information explained the allusion. Rebellious speech, in situations of immediate and violent repression, has to be utterly elusive and must express itself through an almost imperceptible inflection, a stress that is highly ambiguous but that, to those who know, manages to convey smoldering derision. "Yes, *boss*" the bowing slave cries out with a broad grin, and the master may feel entitled to wonder if the man is an idiot, or if he is making a fool of him.

So it does not seem desirable to prove that Bruegel ventured into this field, since any attempt to do so can only lead one into a labyrinth of mirrors. Some writers point out that the Hapsburg eagle is clearly visible on the tabard of the herald in *The Massacre of the Innocents*—a reference, in their view, to the exactions of the Duke of Alva (the painting is undated however, and several historians believe it may have been painted before these events). Be that as it may, the emperor himself does not seem to have given it a second thought, since according to van

Mander (whose book was published in 1604), the painting belonged at that date to the imperial collection in Prague.[4]

More important still, one may well have doubts about the social impact of a satirical work intended to be hung in a private home. As for the drawings Bruegel asked his wife to burn, it does not seem likely, in view of the sensible caution he showed on his deathbed that he ever displayed them to any but a few intimate friends. The point should not so much be to prove that Bruegel made an issue of everyday abuses, but rather to understand in what way his entire production relates to these experiences of daily life. Quite a lot is known about daily life in his day, since numerous documents provided detailed information on the subject. This allows us to have some knowledge of the circumstances in which Bruegel lived and of the events that may have impressed him from day to day. This however, does not mean that we will find direct traces of these events in his work, nor that any given painting should definitely be regarded as a response to some specific event. Bruegel was also, and above all, concerned with the broader field of moral or cultural events; his work responds to this wider context.

In his own day a number of people wrote pamphlets denouncing the belief in witchcraft, the brutal torture of poor confused souls, the rounding up of further victims accused in the torture chambers, the ferocity of an inhuman law and the fiery deaths that it decreed. Yet such writings had *no* decisive effect, nor could their humane reasoning put an end to this strange madness. Surprisingly enough, the great thinkers of the period—Francis Bacon, Hugo Grotius, John Selden, or René Descartes, did not even broach the subject. Does this imply they actually believed in witchcraft? Trevor-Roper raises the question and answers it himself: "Why should they court trouble on a secondary and peripheral issue?" he observes. "On the central issue they were not reticent, and it is in their central philosophy that we must see the battle they were fighting: *a battle*" [the italics are mine] "*that would cause the world of witches, ultimately, to wither away*." (p. 109) This also applies to Bruegel himself and to his work, for his own battles were also being fought at a far deeper level than that of day-to-day events.

A book cannot hope to put out a bonfire—in fact it may well be in danger of being burned itself as long as certain fundamental notions have not been modified. A painting hung in the intimacy of a comfortable home can hardly hope to stir up the masses nor put an end to a reign of terror. If, by mere chance, it should happen to find its way into the emperor's study, the painting may indeed appeal to him as private person. But will he also hear the appeal to the emperor? In such matters, our current perception of such things is no doubt affected by the very existence of art books today. Some forty large volumes have been devoted, in all or in part, to Bruegel. Hundreds of others contain reproduction of his paintings. Bruegel, today, has become a star. In his own time, however, he was just one of the 360 painters of the Guild of Saint

Luke in Antwerp, a discreet citizen, unknown to the crowd, highly regarded by a few select friends. Significantly enough, nobody seems to have thought the facts of Bruegel's life worth recording until Carel van Mander, thirty years after his death, came up with the idea of gathering information on all the Flemish painters since the days of Jan van Eyck.

Here are the main facts he recorded: Bruegel was born in the village of Bruegel near Breda.[5] Historians today assume that this means the village of Brögel, which is in the vicinity of Bree (*Breda* in Latin) in Belgian Limburg. "He studied art in Antwerp with Peter Coeck van Aelst. . . . Thence he went on to study with Jerome Cock" (also in Antwerp) "and after that he traveled through France and Italy. He worked a lot in the vein of Hieronymus Bosch. . . . During his journeys he imitated [*gheconterfeyt*—"counterfeited" in Flemish] numerous views after nature. Indeed, he followed nature so well that one might say he devoured all the mountains and rocks while passing through the Alps and, once he had returned home, spewed them up again onto canvas and wood panels. . . . He chose to live in Antwerp where he settled and was admitted into the guild of painters in the year 1551 of our Lord. He worked a great deal for a merchant by the name of Hans Franckert. Franckert was an excellent and honest man who took pleasure in Bruegel's company and spent much of his time with him every day. Together they would often leave town to visit peasants, or to attend village fairs or weddings, wearing peasant garb. They came to the wedding bearing gifts like everyone else and claiming to be members of the family of the bride or groom. Bruegel took pleasure in studying the appearances of the peasants as they ate, danced, leaped about, or courted on another, as well as in all their other amusements. All these things he later reproduced very cleverly and with greatest of ease, both in tempera and in oil, for he had an exceptional mastery of both techniques. He also knew how to represent these peasant men and women most exactly in the dress of the Campine or some other region, and he depicted their village ways in the most natural and convincing manner, as they danced, or walked, or stood about at rest, or pursued some other activity. He had a marvelous assurance in his representations, and he handled the pen with a great deal of precision and charm when sketching figures from life.

"In Antwerp he live with a servant girl whom he might even have married had she not been rather too sparing of the truth and, in fact, to put it bluntly, a habitual liar. They talked the matter over and came to an agreement: Each time she told a lie, he would make a notch on a wooden pole of reasonable length. And if the notches came to cover the full extent of the pole, their projected wedding would be definitely set aside. This came to pass after quite a short while.

"When the widow of Peter Coeck finally settled in Brussels, Bruegel went there to court her daughter (whom he had so often carried in his arms when she was a little

---

[4] According to Friedländer, Bruegel's paintings may have received the same privilege granted the court fool at the imperial court.

[5] Van Mander spells his name Bruegel. The painter first signed Brueghel then, starting in 1559, Bruegel.

girl and he himself was living in Coeck's house), and he married her. Her mother, however, insisted that Bruegel should leave Antwerp and come to live in Brussels, that he might be separated from his former friend and should forget her. And this was done.

"He was a very quiet and proper man, not talkative, but very fond of joking in company. He would sometimes organize a shindy or some ghostly apparition to frighten people or even his own pupils.

"Some of his best works now belong to the emperor. . . .[6] Shortly before his death the aldermen of Brussels commissioned some paintings representing the digging of the canal from Brussels to Antwerp, but his death prevented this from being done. Many of his bizarre, allegorical, or comical works are found in the form of engravings, but there were also a great number of them, drawn with a clear and sure hand and bearing various inscriptions. When he was already stricken with the disease from which he was to die, he had his wife burn part of these, for he feared they were too mordant and satirical. One may either suppose that he felt remorse, or that he feared that they might cause her some inconvenience if she were held responsible for them.

"In his will he left his wife a painting showing a *Magpie on the Gallows*. . . . He also painted *When Truth Breaks Out* (*daer de waerheyt doorbreeckt*). This, in his own opinion, was his best work."

When Truth Breaks Out—this painting, among others, remains unknown to us. Points of van Mander's narrative, written in a colloquial and colorful Flemish, have been confirmed by documents discovered in various archives. Nothing has been found concerning Bruegel's birth. The archives of the Guild of Saint Luke in Antwerp still exist, however, and they include a list of twenty-two masters (including twelve painters) admitted in 1551. Among them appears the name of "Peeter Brueghels" (the final "s" being a genitive of filiation). We also know that no one was admitted into the Guild before the age of twenty-five—hence Bruegel must have been born around 1525.

His travels through France and Italy can be reconstructed in part, thanks to his works and to various other documents. In 1552, he passed through Lyon. This seems the logical itinerary, and the inventory of the belongings of the Croatian miniaturist Giorgio Glovovic (or Giulio Clovio, 1498–1578), who lived and worked in Rome, includes "*un quadro di Leon di Francia a guazzo* [gouache] *di mano di Maestro Pietro Brugole.*" It seems likely that he then embarked at Marseille and sailed directly to the southern tip of the Italian boot. He saw Reggio of Calabria and did a drawing of its burning by the Turks that occurred precisely in 1552 (though he need not have been there in time to witness the event). He also seems to have visited Messina since his representation of that city is said to be accurate. And since we have taken him this far in our speculation, why not send him on to Palermo, where he might have been taken to see the Palazzo Sclafani. There he would have seen a fresco representing the Triumph of Death, which might conceivably have provided some inspiration for his own *Triumph of Death* painted ten years later (in 1562). Next he sailed north, following the coast. He saw, let us suppose, the fantastical rocks of the Amalfi coast and the city of Naples (of which he painted a view in 1558). In 1553 he continued northward to Rome, where he made friends with Giulio Clovio, the Croatian painter mentioned above. The New York Public Library owns a miniature of the *Last Judgment* by Clovio. A medallion in the border represents a fleet caught in a storm. It is thought today that this was done by young Bruegel. In Rome he must have seen works by Michelangelo and by Raphael. Continuing north he may have visited Assisi (?), Arezzo (?), Florence (most likely), and Bologna (without a doubt). In Bologna he met Scipio Fabius, one of the new breed of geographers that were also beginning to appear in the Netherlands. This we know because of two letters that Fabius wrote to his colleague Abraham Ortels in Antwerp in 1561 and 1565. In both of these he sends his greetings to "Petrus Bruochl."

After Bologna, Bruegel crossed the Alps, keeping a record of his journey in a whole sequence of drawings of fine intensity. He took the Saint Gothard Pass (Rubens owned a painting by Bruegel depicting the pass—it has since been lost), passed through Waltensburg in Switzerland (another drawing) and the village of Rhuis in the Rhine valley ("The Large Rhine Landscape"—a drawing). One cannot definitely establish the date of his return to Antwerp (1554?), but by 1556 he was already working for Jerome Cock, whose shop, The Sign of the Four Winds, thereafter sold prints more or less competently derived from his drawings. One may also suppose that he took a trip to Amsterdam in 1562—three drawings dated that year represent a gate of this city.

Van Mander's narrative is further confirmed by the marriage register of the church of Notre Dame de la Chapelle in Brussels. Under the heading of the year 1563, one may still read the inscription PEETER BRUGELL/ SOLMT/MARYKEN COCKS.

As we have already seen, one of his closest friends was Abraham Ortels, "the most famous geographer of his day," says Charles de Tolnay, who goes on to give a list of Ortels' circle: "Franz Hogenbergh, Christophe Plantin [the famous printer], Jan Rademaker, D. V. Coornhert, Hubert Goltzius, Henry Nicolaes, founder of a religious sect whose ideal was a 'libertine' view in religious matters, and stoicism in one's attitude to life. . . ." "Libertine," is taken here in the sense that the sixteenth

---

[6] Van Mander enumerates *The Tower of Babel, The Massacre of the Innocents,* and *The Conversion of Saint Paul,* all of which belonged to the emperor. Whenever he mentions a painting he also gives the owner's name when he happens to know it.

View of the port of Naples (1558)

The Gates of Amsterdam
(1562)

century gave the term. It means "liberal" or "tolerant." Coornhert, another influential religious thinker then living in Antwerp, was also à libertine in this sense.

Scholars have even come across a faint trace of Bruegel's intimate, the good and honest Hans Franckert. He was a native of Nuremberg, the city of Albrecht Dürer (1471–1528), and, together with Jerome Cock, a member of the Antwerp Chamber of Rhetoric known as "de Violiere" (the Stock-flower). His name can still be found in the registers of this association.

One last document has been found in the minutes of the meeting of the Brussels City Council of January 18, 1569. It states that Master Peeter van Bruegel would be relieved of the obligation of quartering Spanish soldiers. One cannot be entirely sure, however, that this refers to the painter, and not to a doctor of the same name, Magister Bruegelius, who also lived in Brussels at that time.

In any event, Bruegel died that same year, on the fifth of September. Little more than this can be ascertained about his life.

Works by Peter Bruegel The Elder Reproduced in this Book

MAGDALENA POENITENS·

3. PENITENT MARY MAGDELENE *(1558) Copperplate engraving, 36.5 × 42.8 cm, published by J. Cock in 1559.*

Ghy heden van Mallegem wilt nu wel syn gesint   Om v te genesen ben ick gecomen hier.   Compt vry den meesten met den minsten sonder verbeyen
Ick Vrou Hexe wil hier oock wel worden bemint   Tiuwen dinste met myn onder meesteryssen fier   Hebby de wesp int hooft. oft loteren v de krjen.

4. THE WITCH OF MALLEGHEM *Copperplate engraving, 35.5 × 48 cm, published by J. Cock in 1559.*

5. THE BATTLE OF THE SAFES AND THE MONEY BOXES
Copperplate engraving published by J. Cock in 1558.

Aux quatre Vents   P. Bruegel Inuēt

Quid modo diuitiæ, quid fulci vasta metalli   Jllecebræ inter tantas, atq agmina furum,   Prçda facit furem, feruens mala cura ministrat
Congesta numini æris referta nouis;   Inditum cunctis efferris, Sincui erit,   Impetus, et spoliis apta rapina feris.
Tis al om gelt en goet, dit stryden en twisten   Al siemen v oni andri, wildt met gheluiten   Maer soeckt wel alst om om te verdooien,
                                                                                                                Vairem quari wy den haet die ons neyt en mist,   Maer men souwer niet krygen, woerder niet te roouen.

I. – The Sign of the Four Winds

Campagnola, Landscape

Landscape with St. Jerome
(1558)

Young Bruegel returned from his Italian journey brimming over with visions of the world's immensity. It may seem obvious to us that an artist should want to depict nature. But this has not always been the case. The most fundamental concern of art has not always been to inventory the sights of the world or present its more *spectacular* aspect. Artists have been more inclined to pay attention to the *meaning* of the world and of life—to the intention underlying all things. Even now, art in its most serious forms is involved in this pursuit. If young Bruegel chose to turn his attention to the awe-inspiring landscapes he saw with his own eyes during his journeys, it was clearly because the scope, the power, the cold grandeur and mild gentleness of the earth, and its ability to arouse strong emotions, seemed enigmatic to him—a reality calling for some reflection.[1] Some twenty-five drawings of real, imaginary, or composite landscapes by Bruegel are known to us today. They date from his years of travels or were later inspired by the vivid memories of a time when the world unfolded before him in its breathtaking beauty.

The Italian cities do not appear to have moved him to draw; nor, for that matter, did the great painterly blooming of the Renaissance. Yet he was obviously attentive to the lessons of the Italian painters. Some were instantly assimilated (Campagnola, for instance, affected his treatment of landscapes). Others, chiefly those of Michelangelo, would only begin to be applied fifteen years later, after they had matured in the deeper cellars of his mind.

It appears that a job was already awaiting Bruegel when he returned to Antwerp. According to van Mander, he had worked for Jerome Cock before his departure. Cock was a painter turned art dealer whose landscape style is believed to have influenced Bruegel to a certain extent. It may well have been Cock who urged him to undertake the journey south. He had gone there himself in his day. When he decided to turn to the art trade, Cock opened a shop called The Sign of the Four Winds. There he produced and sold engravings drawn from the works of his brother Matthys (another artist whose landscapes are

[1] See chapter IV.

thought to have influenced Bruegel) and by other artists, including Bruegel himself.

The drawings Bruegel did in the course of his travels ultimately yielded a number of landscape prints. Some ten of these have survived to this day, including an imaginary one, *Penitent Mary Magdalene*, and another, *Landscape with Saint Jerome*, with Saint Jerome tucked away in a corner of the broad perspective. It was probably Cock who first introduced Bruegel, with infectious enthusiasm, to the works of Hieronymus Bosch when the young artist returned from Italy. It may be that Cock, like any other sensible businessman, sensed that there was an untapped market here. Thus it was that Bruegel, in 1556 and at the age of thirty-one, threw himself wholeheartedly into the exploration of a realm of allegorical fantasy—just as he had, until then, explored the realm of geographical reality. True, he borrowed abundantly from the idiom of Bosch, but he used it in an entirely different spirit. While Bosch's paintings express a constant anguish (the anguish of a person overwhelmed by his visions), Bruegel shows himself to be a man of great warmth and attentive sympathy and, above all, an acute observer of the human comedy, endowed with all the benevolent detachment this requires. Bosch painted the landscapes of his own psyche—Bruegel did not. Despite the apparent similarities, Bruegel's language is more didactic and, on closer scrutiny, it turns out to be surprisingly "distanced" in the Brechtian sense. This is particularly apparent in the series of drawings devoted to the seven deadly sins. Bruegel's demons are not the embodiment of some nocturnal terror; they are not bred from the cold sweat of angst. The situations they illustrate are neither inevitable nor definitive. They do not even betray some inclination to frighten or dismay the viewer. On the contrary, all of these works appear to arise out of a desire to stimulate reflection, in a spirit close to that of Stoicism. "Travel will not solve your problems," Seneca declares in substance in a letter to his friend Lucilius, "for you cannot leave your own self behind." Bosch's monsters reappear in Bruegel's works, but under a highly rationalized and ironical guise. Even in his "Temptation of Saint Anthony," a subject Bruegel dealt with in a markedly Boschian idiom in 1556, the monsters fail to convey the insinuatingly evil persistence that characterizes them in the original. In Bruegel's works, such monstrous visions usually strike one as merely droll or ludicrous. In his "Temptation of Saint Anthony" real emotion appears to be focalized in two points only: in the features of the saint, who does indeed look sorely tried, and in the face of the man who, at the center of the print, is being thrown off a cliff.

The series *The Seven Deadly Sins* was begun in 1556 and completed in 1557 with a final print depicting the Last Judgment. At first glance the concept of the series might be thought medieval. An allegorical figure embodying one of the vices stands at the center of each print. Around this figure scenes unfold that are meant to illustrate the nefarious consequences of this particular vice. Each print is literally crawling with monsters large and small, but their appearance is each time derived from reflection on the matter at hand, from free association, and from familiar turns of phrase that Bruegel enjoys taking literally. Thus, for instance, in the print *Avarice*, an enormous pair of shears can be seen closing upon a naked figure. The explanation is simple enough: In every age and every language people have been sheared, trimmed, and fleeced. *Gluttony* shows, among other things, a man carrying his tremendous gut about on a wheelbarrow. *Lust* includes some female figures (or devils), wearing a two-horned headdress, which, we are told, was the sign of the bawd, but also dogs, monkeys, and cocks (animals notoriously expeditious in their lechery), and a huge mussel because of its obvious ressemblance to female genitalia. *Pride*, among other figures, includes a peacock; *Envy*, two dogs quarreling over a bone, and *Sloth*, some snails and a huge slug. In *Envy* one also encounters the literal transcription of a familiar Flemish phrase. People can be seen trying on shoes; a grotesque devil is shown devouring one; a woman in a basket is weeping, apparently because she has not managed to sell any of hers. This, it would seem, alludes to an expression touching upon one's social position, one's standing or "footing."

All these works are meant to point a moral. In their similarity with the nineteenth-century picture puzzle known as a rebus they may strike one as rather laborious. But despite the first impression, despite the seemingly familiar repertory of figures and phrases, the spirit and mind-set from which they are derived are no longer medieval. The torments depicted do not take place in the nether region of Hell whose topography found its definitive form in the writings of Dante. In Bruegel's work, instead they stand before one as an allegorical representation of life in the present world. The prints are intended to illustrate the experience of a soul dominated by some haunting obsession, and they already foreshadow a rather more modern psychological outlook that implies that every vice is in itself a torment.

Two scholars (Fritz Grossman and Carl Gustav Stridbeck) have shown that the imagery of this series, and more explicitly still their inscriptions in Latin and Flemish, reflect the "libertine" (i.e., liberal or tolerant) religious view formulated in the writings of D. V. Coornhert. It so happens that Coornhert was himself an engraver and a member, like Bruegel, of the circle of friends surrounding the geographer Abraham Ortels.[2]

According to Grossman and Stridbeck these inscriptions, which appear in Latin and Flemish beneath the prints, and in Flemish only (in handwriting that is not Bruegel's) under the drawings, are paraphrases of the writings of Coornhert. Consequently, and despite their Boschian or medieval imagery, these prints should be seen as the expression of a new religious outlook that no longer threatens the sinner with eternal damnation, but implies that every vice is an aberration that causes suffering in this life.

Our understanding of the details of these works is probably restricted by an irredeemable ignorance of many aspects of idiomatic Flemish of the period. We may assume that a kindly, unsardonic humor was not foreign to their conception. But they also reflect some measure of emotion, though it is usually kept in the background. Here one comes across little vignettes that already seem to carry the seeds of romantic symbolism: In *Sloth*, the figures with legs apparently trapped in the lethargy of stagnant waters as they stand gazing upon the arm whose monitory index on the clock face points at the hour of some final opportunity; in *Envy*, the vignette depicting a shipwreck, or the funeral with its hooded mourners; in *Wrath*, the pointless battle around a ship of fools poised on two enormous barrels; in *Lust*, the huge and vicious perch leaping out of the moat and grasping a victim by the leg while others scatter across the bridge; and finally, behind the allegorical figure of *Pride*, the sinister crew of pimps and bawds surrounding a naked, panic-stricken girl.

Other works stand closer to this series in time, but it may be more appropriate at this stage to examine the parallel series of the *Seven Virtues* begun in 1559 (Bruegel was then thirty-four) and completed the following year. Here we discover a different kind of world. With a single exception, *Fortitude*[3], the demons and monsters are gone.

Sloth (detail)

Envy (detail)

---

[2] Religious liberalism had also played a part in the young life of Ortels, whose father, in 1535, suffered some difficulties for wanting to translate the new English Bible into Flemish.

[3] And Patience, but this eighth "virtue" (1557) was not part of the series.

The allegorical figure, which now represents a virtue, is still found standing in the middle. But around it appear scenes from daily life that are intended to illustrate the beneficial effects of each virtue. Here, even more than in the series on the vices, Bruegel's real opinions are cloaked in seeming indifference. One may indeed be tempted to read a savage irony into certain aspects of these prints—an irony comparable to that of Jonathan Swift.

At first glance everything looks pretty conventional. The print devoted to *Faith* represents men busily preaching and distributing the sacraments; *Charity* offers a survey of the corporal works of mercy: feeding the hungry, clothing the naked, visiting prisoners and the sick, welcoming strangers, burying the dead; *Prudence* depicts various acts of practical foresight; *Temperance* is a repertory of the arts and sciences. All these scenes bespeak a practical, down-to-earth mentality, of the kind one might expect to encounter in a Flemish society composed mostly of traders. The print entitled *Faith*, however, raises a certain number of questions, particularly if we assume that Bruegel shared Coornhert's views—for the latter, according to Grossman, favored "a personal relationship to God that *dispenses with the external ceremonies of the churches* (Catholic, Lutheran or Calvinist), and a moral philosophy that dwells on man's duty to overcome sin into which he is drawn by his own foolishness." But if this is indeed Bruegel's opinion, how are we to interpret this print? *Hope* also presents aspects that can strike one as ironic: Men are shown scattered over the sea, their hair standing on end with terror. Some can be seen clutching at floating debris as they stare wide-eyed at the gaping maws of a monstrous fish. Meanwhile, on the dock a portly figure complacently observes the scene, hands joined as though in prayer. On the other side some unfortunate prisoners are praying for deliverance. In the middle however, and as though in contrast, more active folk are shown energetically fighting a fire, and in the distance, peasants can be seen tirelessly tilling the soil.

The most problematic work in the series is devoted to the virtue of *Justice*. The allegorical figure stands blindfolded, as tradition requires, to ensure her impartiality. But what *is* being hidden from her sight in the present case? Not the power or indigence of the petitioner, but an inventory of various forms of torture, barbarous punishments, beheadings, hangings, and burnings at the stake. Our modern sensibility may be tempted to protest: What kind of justice is that? And where does Bruegel himself stand on this point? Surely this could not have been his idea of the proper administration of justice. All the rest of his work suggests that he derived no pleasure from the sight of the gallows.

The artist who, in *The Way to Calvary*, contrasted the insensitive excitement of the crowd and the sorrow of the saints, seems to have taken another view of such matters. But then, how is one to understand the series of the Virtues taken as a whole? First, one should bear in mind the circumstances under which these works were produced. Bruegel was then working under the vigilant eye of the "Thought Police." The prints were published in 1560 or shortly thereafter. Philip II's fiercest "placards"

Wrath (detail)

Pride (detail)

had already been put into effect, and the artist had to avoid the sort of slip that might have led Jerome Cock, together with his engravers and Bruegel himself, to one of the nasty fates illustrated here. The print devoted to *Justice* bears a Latin inscription according to which "the purpose of the law is either, by means of punishment, to correct the person who receives it, or to better others by his example, or to protect the community and overcome evil." Having thus taken his precautions as far as the authorities were concerned, Bruegel and his friends could speak their minds in presence of people they trusted. One may suppose, in fact, that the figure of justice in this print is blind to the inhumanity of her own representatives.

This series is also completed by a final print on a different subject, *Christ in Limbo*. This refers to a tradition according to which Christ, after his death and before his resurrection, descended into Limbo (or into Hell), in order to free all those who had been awaiting him there since Adam's fall. The gates of the infernal prison have been shattered and the just are shown walking out of the mouth of Hell, raising their arms toward the bubble of light that surrounds the triumphant Christ and separates him from the impenetrable night and the monsters of Hell. Should this be taken to imply that Christ also delivers the just from the alienation, the "hell" of precisely such a representation of the virtues as we discover here in all the other prints? The point might well be argued, for all the plates of the series were intended to be seen as a coherent whole, and they should be interpreted in that light.

"The Ass at School" (1556) expresses some of the feelings the state of education might have provoked in a thoughtful person. There are reminiscences here of the writings of Sebastian Brant (*The Ship of Fools*), of Desiderius Erasmus, and no doubt of François Rabelais, whose *Gargantua* had been published in 1534. The scene depicts a turbulent classroom. The master is giving a troublesome boy a spanking. The ass, whose figure dominates the scene, is studying a sheet of music. The Latin inscription stresses the obvious: "Send him to Paris if you wish, but if he is an ass here at home, he isn't likely to become a horse in some other city." Yet Bruegel's drawing is not devoid of ambiguity. For one thing all the schoolboys have the faces of adults: They represent monks, lawyers, doctors, and other types of supposedly learned persons. But they are not learning anything in the classroom, and in due course (Bruegel implies), they will all make good use of the authority conferred upon them by their diplomas to stultify or swindle their clients, or medicate them to death. The print offers a blend of the vigorous criticism of old-style education voiced by Rabelais and the instinctive suspicion felt by uneducated people in presence of the "learned." As in so many other works by Bruegel, a surprising variety of things are going on, and behind a grating, one can once again make out the distanced observer, the accomplice and prompter of our own judgment.

"Big Fish Eat Little Fish" (1556) and *The Battle of the Safes and the Money Boxes* (1558?) must have seemed entirely topical when J. Cock first published them in Antwerp. The city, one of the capitals of banking and finance, had gone through an unprecedented general bankruptcy in 1557. The emperor had immediately decreed a financial moratorium, and even the city government had found this necessary.

"Big Fish Eat Little Fish" is a straightforward illustration of the axiom referred to in the title. The print published by Cock was, for some reason, attributed to Hieronymus Bosch. It may have been no more than a commercial ploy, or again, Bruegel might actually have sought his inspiration in a work by Bosch that has since been lost. If the latter is indeed the case, then Bruegel has clearly left his distinctive mark on the print itself. The helmeted figure armed with a large knife shown opening the belly of the largest fish also appears (accompanied by an identical twin) in the print illustrating the effects of *Wrath*. On one side a squatting figure holds a fishing pole and uses a little fish for bait. "You must use little fish to catch the bigger ones," the proverb intones. The inevitable figure of the witness is, in this instance, the man in a boat pointing out the central scene to his child: A giant fish has been washed up on the shore, and a mass of smaller fish can be seen pouring out of his slit belly, whereas in turn, etc. *The Battle of the Safes and the Money Boxes* (one might just as well say "the battle of banking and of savings") is quite as literal in its presentation (note the metaphorical double boat hook on the flags). The money boxes are the pear-shaped figures. This was a familiar shape for such objects, and we shall come across it again in *The Battle of Carnival and Lent*, where the same pear-shaped boxes are used to collect alms.

After having completed his series devoted to the seven deadly sins, and before dealing with the virtues, Bruegel turned out drawings for three prints touching upon the classic theme of human folly: *Everyman* (*Elck* in Flemish), *The Alchemist*, and *The Witch of Malleghem* (or *The Stone of Madness*). This last work, a print based on an original drawing that has been lost, clearly shows how Bruegel's wit could occasionally be reduced to mere

vulgarity at the hand of a less competent etcher. The subject is a familiar one and occurs, for instance, in the works of Hieronymus Bosch. Quack doctors, whose technique was comparable to that of certain surgeons now practicing their sleight of hand in the Philippines, would offer to cure madness by surgically removing from the patient's skull a stone that caused the illness. One of them (like similar figures in Bosch's paintings) has a funnel set upside down on his head. The "Malleghem" referred to in the title is a real place name, but it appears here as a play on words whose connotations might be rendered by a term like "Crazy-town."

The tone becomes both stranger and more serious in the print entitled *Elck* (*Everyman*). Anxious old men, some of them holding lanterns, can be seen searching through a desperate jumble of wares and occasionally quarreling over some piece of cloth. The ever-present witness is, in this case, no more than a picture hanging from the wall. It represents a man sitting on a large pile of junk and looking at himself in a mirror: "No man knows himself," an inscription on the bottom of the frame declares. *The Alchemist* is a splendid and complex print, fairly easy to understand. It depicts a ragged and emaciated practitioner of the mysterious art, busying himself with his ovens and alembics. A Fool kneels beside him, fanning the embers. The Fool represents the alchemist's driving folly, which will ultimately lead to ruin. The man's wife shakes out her purse and discovers it is empty. Their hungry children clamber to the cupboard in search of food and find nothing but an empty pot, which one of them puts over his head like a helmet. The witness is there too, to point the obvious moral. With one hand he designates the scene, with the other a book on which we make out the word ALGHEMIST— "alchemist," no doubt, but also AL GHEMIST (which in Flemish means "all messed up"). The background of the print relates the end of the alchemist's tale. The entire family (with one of the children still wearing the cooking pot on his head) is shown approaching an almshouse. A nun comes out to receive them. The conclusion is not so far removed from that of the series on the Vices: Every vice (or folly) holds its own punishment.

The Skaters Before Saint George's Gate (1559) is a purely humorous print of skaters going about their sometimes awkward sport. Pedestrians, their feet on firm ground, observe them with malicious grins. The engraver added a trilingual inscription: "*lubricitas humanae vitae— la lubricité de la vie humain—de slibberachtigheyt van's menschen leven*," which is merely a heavy-handed pun ("the lubricity/slipperiness of human life") based on the fact that the Latin term *lubricitas* implies both "slipperiness" (as in "lubricant") and lubricity in the erotic sense. *The Kermess in Hoboken* (1559), finally, offers Bruegel's first encyclopedic overview of peasant life.

6. THE TEMPTATION OF SAINT ANTHONY (1556) *Ink drawing, 21.6 × 32.6 cm (reproduced in original dimensions).*

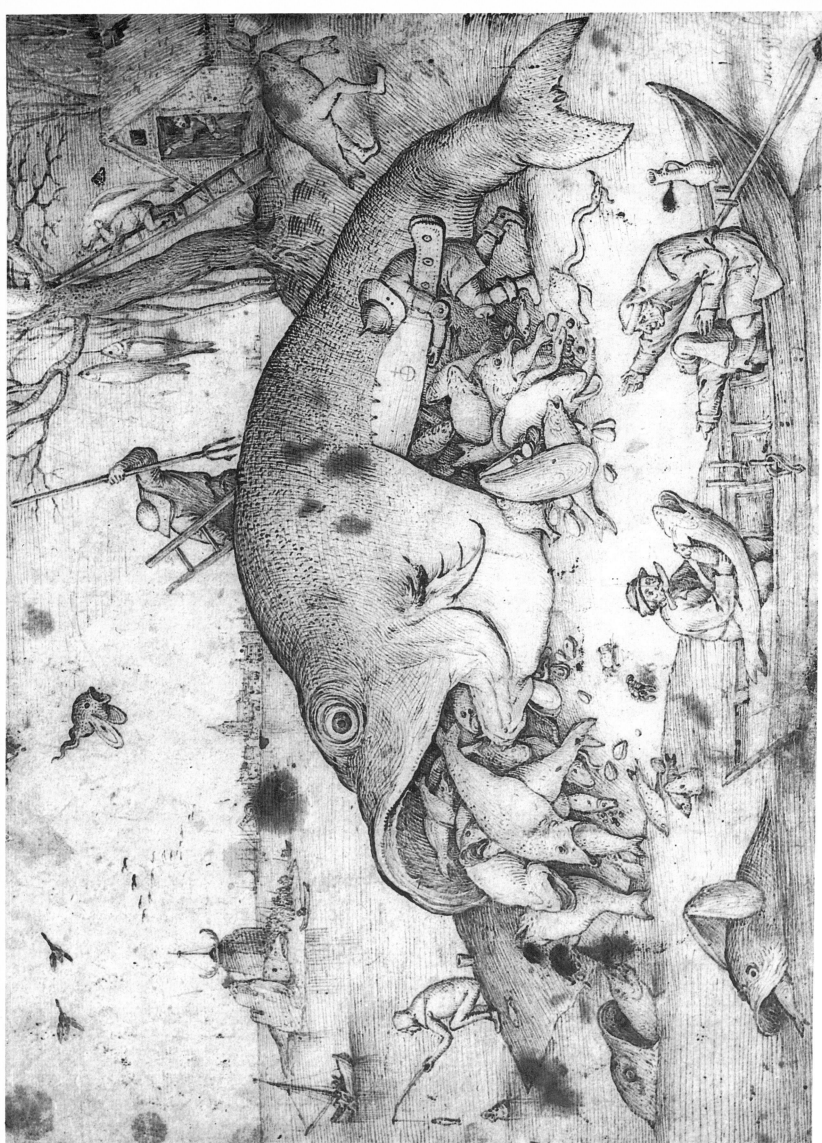

7. BIG FISH EAT LITTLE FISH (1556) *Ink drawing, 21.6 × 32.6 cm (reproduced in original dimensions).*

18. IRA (WRATH) *(1557) Ink drawing, 22 × 30 cm.*

19. INVIDIA (ENVY) *(1557) Ink drawing, 22 × 30 cm.*

20. DESIDIA (SLOTH) *(1557) Ink drawing, 21.4 × 29.6 cm.*

21. THE LAST JUDGMENT *(1558) Ink drawing, 23 × 29.9 cm.*

22. FIDES (FAITH) *(1559) Ink drawing, 22.6 × 29.5 cm.*

23. CARITAS (CHARITY) *(1559) Ink drawing, 22.4 × 29.3 cm.*

24. PRUDENTIA (PRUDENCE) (1559) Ink drawing, 22.4 × 29.9 cm.

25. SPES (HOPE) (1559) Ink drawing, 22.4 × 29.5 cm.

26. JUSTICIA (JUSTICE) *(1559) Ink drawing, 22.4 × 29.5 cm.*

27. FORTITUDO (FORTITUDE) *(1560) Ink drawing, 22.4 × 29.3 cm.*

28. TEMPERANTIA (TEMPERANCE) *(1560) Ink drawing, 22 × 29.5 cm.*

29. CHRIST IN LIMBO *(1561) Ink drawing, 22.4 × 29.2 cm.*

II. – Of Carnival and Carnage

All Bruegel's production up to this point can be viewed as no more than prelude. The power of vision and eloquence within him, not yet revealed, would shortly make itself known. The artist had only ten more years of life before him, and it is within this surprisingly short time span that he would produce all his major work as a painter. A few of his paintings, though uncertain in date, must be considered prior to this period (at least one of them was done in 1553), but only in the uncontested works done after 1559 does the painter reveal the full scope of his original and lively genius.

"In all his works," his friend Ortels declared a few years after Bruegel's death—"weeping (*lugens*) as he spoke," says the Latin text—"there was always more reflection than there was painting." Throughout his lifetime, Bruegel undeniably followed his own independent way and the thread of his own thoughts. We have seen that as a young man he journeyed to the wellspring of the art of his day. Hardly an artist in his city, no matter how Flemish he might be, failed to paint with an Italian accent. Paintings were full of colonnades, swirling draperies, rhetorical gestures, and handsome faces devoid of inner life; all this proved the artist to be a man of social distinction and true refinement. Bruegel had gone to drink from the same spring, after which he returned to Antwerp, a city that, according to Francesco Guicciardini, a contemporary witness, could only be compared with Venice. A fine career awaited him. Yet he disdained to follow the wide and easy path. The landscapes he had walked through, the faces he saw every day, did not bear the marks of any Italian style. Bruegel was a confirmed individualist. He stored up all the sights he saw, turned them over in his mind, and tried to penetrate their meaning. He had both the gift of earnestness and the gift of humor. He grasped things from within, understanding what happens inside a body when it is involved in some task and in the continuous effort it requires. But he also knew how to see things from afar, the better to grasp the breadth of this world of which each man sees only a narrow part as he bends his head and body over his labor. Each thing in itself is earnest, but each thing also deserves to be viewed from a certain distance. The world of nature and of man is marked by a wild proliferation, and at the heart of this proliferation, Bruegel sensed a madness at work. This is not mere hyperbole. Our own age has encountered the same thing in another form, and this similarity of experience no doubt allows us to perceive something in Bruegel's work that former centuries, more secure in their convictions than we manage to be, failed to notice. By "madness" I mean an uncontrolled and self-devouring irrationality, a desire that fails to understand its own nature and appears to be bent upon destruction. This is something

Parable of the Sower (1557)

we have encountered in the political and cultural realm in our own century.

In order to make our way through the work that stands before us now like one of the painter's own landscapes in its vast complexity, we need not abide by a strict chronological order, for in doing so, we might well lose sight of deeper coherences. Precisely because this body of paintings is utterly original and personal, it can only be fully understood by following the development of Bruegel's own perception of the world. This approach holds true even if the paintings and their subject matter are the result of a succession of unconnected commissions. Viewed as a continuous discourse, the body of his work expresses this deeper perception. One must approach it as an evolving organic structure. The thematic material will show itself to be as coherently interwoven as the motives of a work of music—so much so that the occasionally random element is swept up in the general movement and loses all independent significance.

The subjects Bruegel chose to deal with in his first paintings are entirely typical of those then favored by engravers. Painting, until then, had been surrounded with a tremendous aura. It was the privileged medium of religious subjects and elevated allegory, and it also served to commemorate crucial events in the lives of princes. A copperplate print was quite another matter. The large number of identical copies, their modest price and small size made engravings a convenient vehicle for less important or elevated matters. Both *The Skaters* and *The Kermess* had been conceived for this medium. Bruegel could very well have done as much with such subjects as *The Flemish Proverbs*, *Children's Games*, or *The Battle of Carnival and Lent*. All these works are characterized by the same mind-set and centerless form of composition that appeared suited to a medium less costly and less noble in purpose than painting. Even if he was not the first nor the only one to do this sort of thing, Bruegel made an important choice when he decided to deal with such subjects in painting. For he inevitably lent a new dignity to his subject to the extent that the medium itself was bound to have such an effect. Not everyone shared his feeling in such matters, to be sure. Several centuries

Twelve proverbs (detail)

would yet elapse before Charles Perrault in France, and the Grimm brothers in Germany, could gain acceptance for the idea that products of the popular imagination were worthy of serious scrutiny. Some people found Bruegel's approach perplexing and could only dispel the feeling by declaring that he was no more than a facile entertainer. Such terms as "Peter the Droll," the "Peasant Bruegel," and even the deplorable epithet "Breugelian" (used to designate the coarse gluttony and drunken vitality of the lower classes) reflect a resolve to ignore the deeper significance of Bruegel's decision. This is not meant to imply that his paintings aren't funny. But the humor they express is that of the universal (which the painted picture inevitably tends to embody) when it takes upon itself the idiosyncratic burden of particularity as does, for instance, Charlie Chaplin's Tramp. Bruegel's humor confronts us with the tough, pathetic drollery of an existence charged with violent, desperate impulses and hemmed in, restrained, and baffled by dark, brutal, and confused circumstances. Such was the familiar world of peasants and burghers in a troubled age. Bruegel's imitators, including his own sons, would all too often be content to copy the outward appearance of his work (with the obvious awkwardness of those who imitate an attitude rather than share an intention), and in this way they would utterly reverse his meaning. Aside from the Le Nain brothers, the seventeenth- and eighteenth-century painters of *gueuseries* (representations of beggars, destitute peasants, and paupers) expressed little more than benign indifference for the unfortunate subjects they portrayed with mutilated limbs or twisted features and dressed in picturesque rags. Unwilling to grasp the *meaning* implicit in their regard of the world and their fellow man, painters and their public chose to reduce it all to mere *spectacle*. It was simpler to view human misery as merely "picturesque."

Bruegel, for his part (and rather like Rabelais, who took such delight in inventories of every kind), discovered peculiar treasures in this subject matter, and in the period of dramatic social change into which he had been born, he chose to undertake the catalogue of a heritage: the wealth of everyday speech and its idiosyncratic flavor; the effervescence of childhood whose imaginative powers burst, like a rush of bubbles, in the face of even the grimmest existence; the catalogue, finally, of adult cele-

brations. The latter are approached with a measure of philosophical dissatisfaction, however, that can be sensed in a work like *The Battle of Carnival and Lent* and that only vanishes when we come to the last great paintings.

The first two big works, *The Flemish Proverbs* (1559) and *Children's Games* (1560), do not really call for much comment. Both are inventories, such as can be found in Rabelais (and, as far as the proverbs are concerned, in the poetry François Villon). The first of these paintings illustrates Flemish proverbs and idiomatic phrases: "to stop up the well after the calf has drowned," "to catch eels by the tail," "to beat one's head against the wall," "to shit on the world," "to mistake horse droppings for figs," "to throw money out of the window" (in Flemish: into the water), "to sit down between two chairs" (and, the Flemish version adds, with one's bottom in the ashes) . . . As for the children's games, since all of them are still in current use today, they don't really call for any explanation. One art historian at least spent some enjoyable hours identifying no fewer than eighty-four of them.

The Battle of Carnival and Lent (1559) does, on the other hand, reward further exploration. Like the two foregoing paintings, it is done on a very large panel (118 × 164.5 cm), but here a more definite and orderly composition begins to bring some structure into the swirling chaos characteristic of the other two works. The general disposition of this work is that of a round or ring around which several "vanishing points" have been placed in a way that creates a diagonal structure. The conception is both medieval and modern, both allegorical and realistically down-to-earth. Dividing the work down the middle, we consistently find references to Carnival (or Mardi Gras), its celebrations and attributes, on the left-hand side, to Lent on the right. To the left there is a tavern, to the right, the church; gluttony is opposed to abstinence; meat, to fish, etc. At the same time the picture is a synthetic presentation of events at nightfall during a carnival celebration in the streets of a small town. In big cities things were more elaborate: Complex floats, designed and built throughout the foregoing year, were driven through the streets either on wheeled platforms or on the kind of sled represented by Bruegel.

Shrove Tuesday (Mardi Gras) is the last day of Carnival preceding the forty days of Lent during which Christians were required to abstain from eating meat (abstinence) and even from eating their fill (fast). This period of privation was a discipline intended to prepare the faithful for the annual commemoration of the death of Christ. It was also an incitation to reflect on sin and death. The roots of Carnival, on the other hand, reach far beyond the Christian era. Its celebrations, with their pre-Christian reminiscences, quite naturally found a niche in the days preceding Lent. A number of more recent traditions gradually attached themselves to these celebrations, and Bruegel gives a sampling of them in the various bands and masquerades shown parading through the streets.

Carnival is personified here by the fattest man in the village. He sits astride a barrel and awkwardly balances a terrine of potted meat on his head. A tournament is beginning, and Carnival has been armed with a large

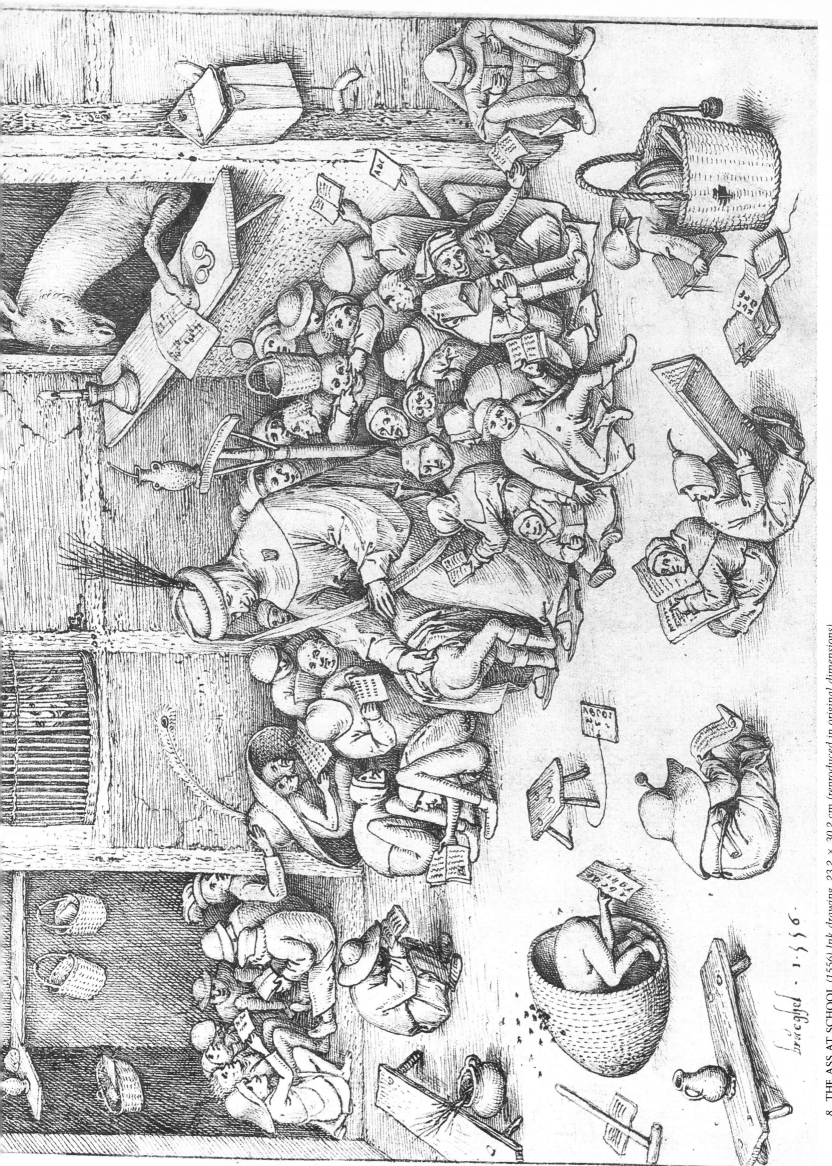

8. THE ASS AT SCHOOL (1556) Ink drawing, 23.2 × 30.2 cm (reproduced in original dimensions).

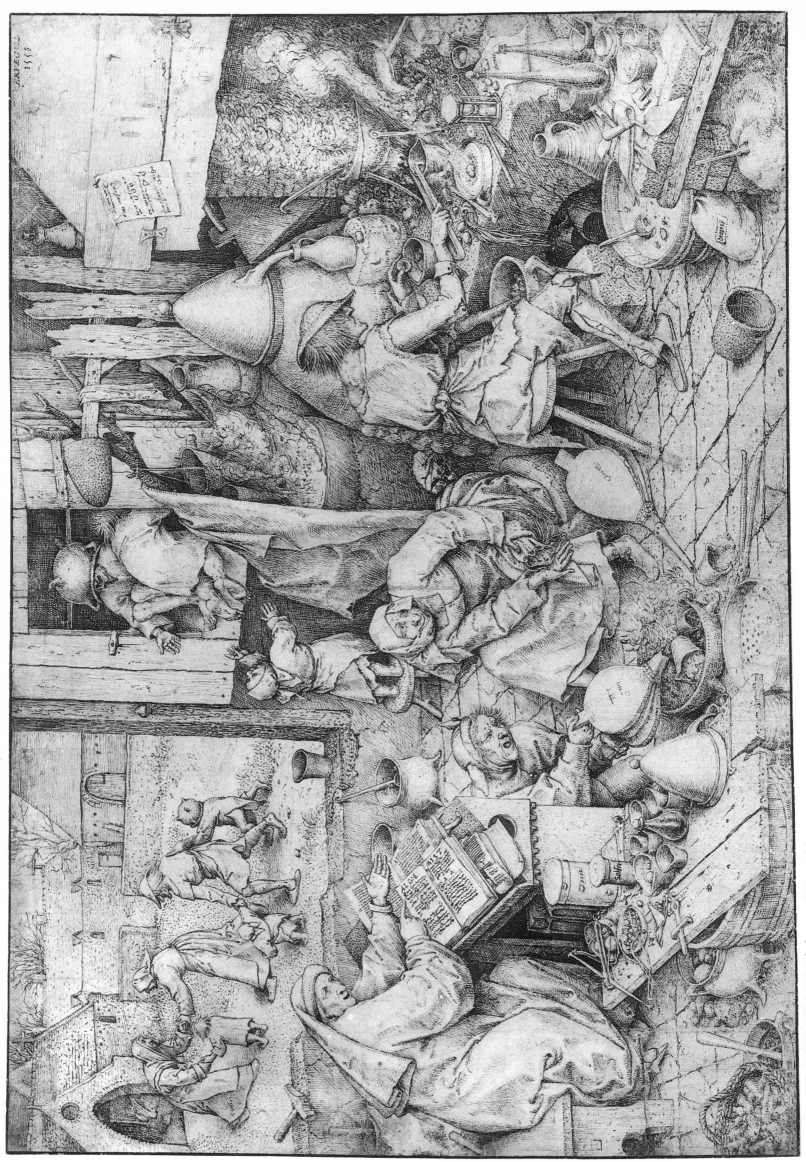

9. THE ALCHEMIST (1558) *Ink drawing, 30.8 × 45.3 cm.*

10. THE ALCHEMIST *Copperplate engraving by van der Heyden after a drawing by Peter Bruegel, about 1558–1559.*

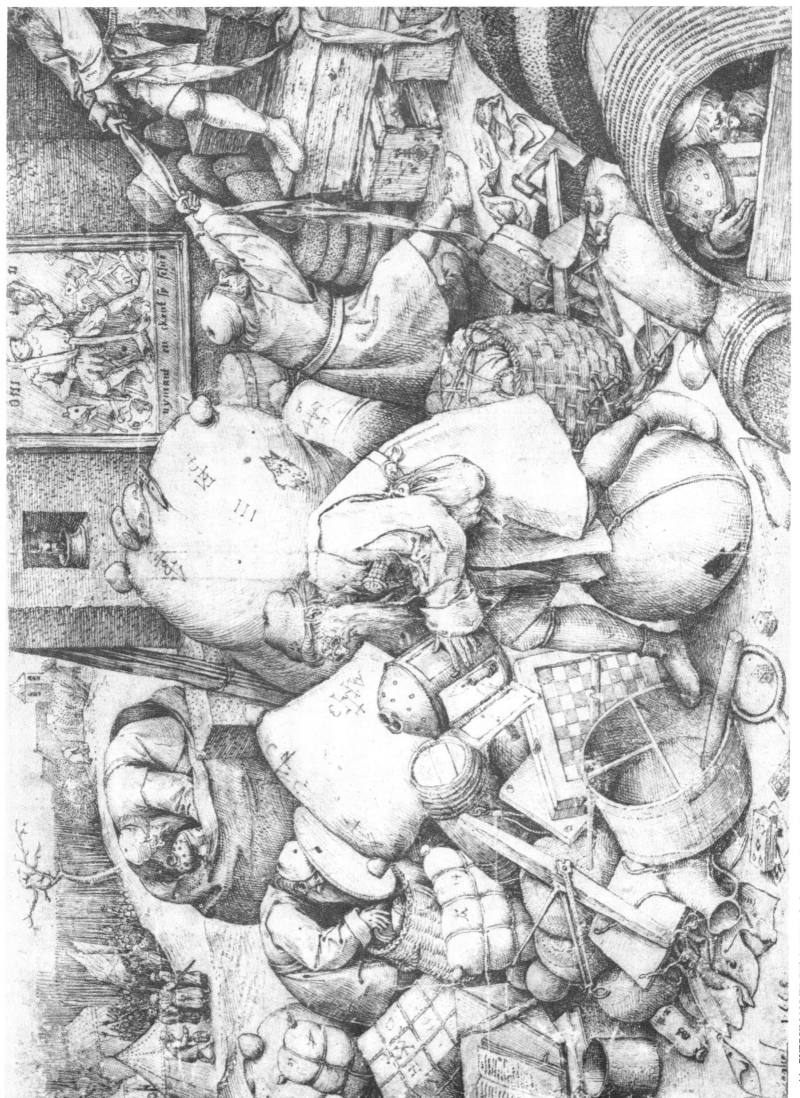

11. EVERYMAN (ELCK) (1558) Ink drawing, 21 × 29.3 cm (reproduced in original dimensions).

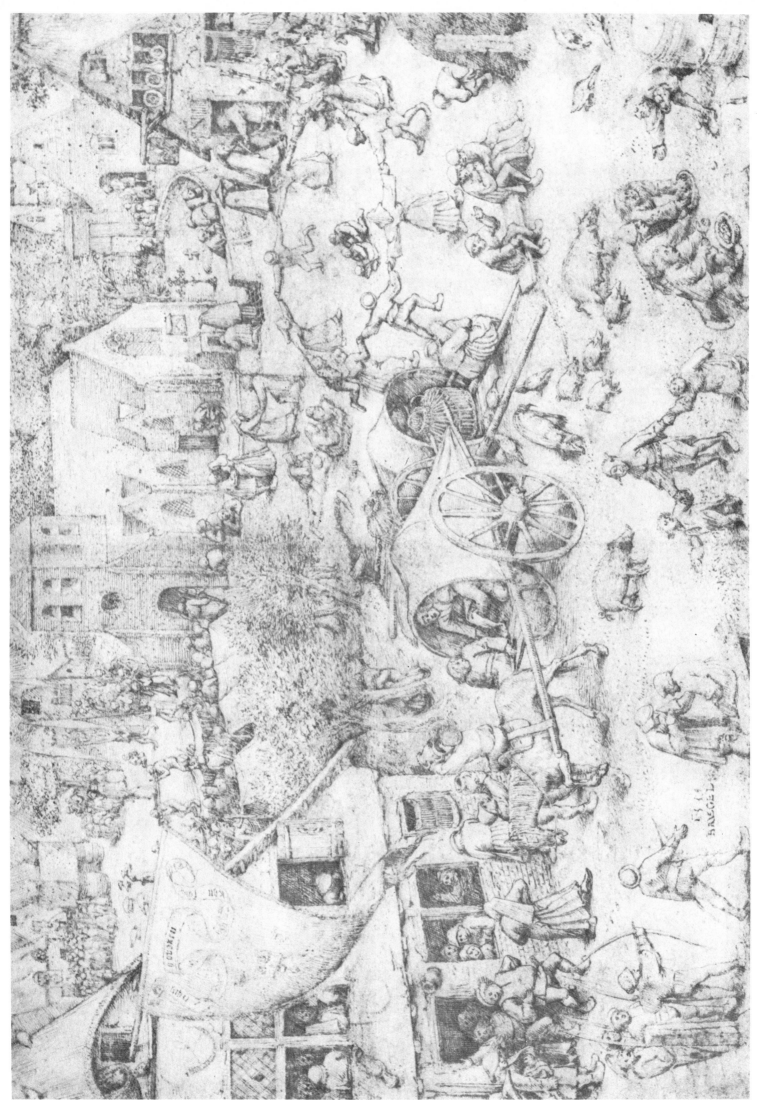

12. THE KERMESS OF HOBOKEN (1559) *Ink drawing, 26.6 × 39.4 cm (reproduced in original dimensions).*

13. THE FALL OF THE MAGICIAN (1564) Ink drawing, 22.3 × 29.2 cm (reproduced in original dimensions).

14. AVARITIA (AVARICE) *(1556) Ink drawing, 23 × 30.2 cm.*

15. GULA (GLUTTONY) *(1557) Ink drawing, 23 × 30.2 cm.*

16. SUPERBIA (PRIDE) *(1557) Ink drawing, 23 × 30 cm.*

17. LUXURIA (LECHERY) *(1557) Ink drawing, 22.6 × 29.7 cm.*

skewer in lieu of a lance. He is surrounded by masks and musicians still typical of carnival today. Lent, on the other hand, is personified by a man so gaunt that one may assume he was released from the almshouse for the occasion. He is seated on a prayer stool, wears a beehive in lieu of a hat (representing "the accumulated honey of spiritual merit"?) and is armed with a wooden shovel on which two dried herrings have been placed. He is followed by children who can be seen shaking the sort of rattles that, in the course of Lent, make their dry, grim sound heard in churches until the bells are allowed to ring once more on Easter morning.

To the left, immediately behind Carnival's escort, is a group depicting the wedding of Mopsus and Nisa, also known as the Filthy Bride. The subject is a rather unexpected variation on Virgil's Eighth Eclogue, for it is merely a coincidence that *Mops*, in Flemish, should mean a country simpleton. As a result of this, however, Mopsus, the worthy, classic shepherd of Virgil's Arcadia, is turned into a good-tempered (and by no means ragged) peasant who takes for wife a grotesque Nisa dressed in rags, wearing a colander on her head, and with her hair done like a magpie's nest. The couple's sole abode is a sheet full of holes thrown over some branches, and the only music for their wedding dance is provided by a knife rattling against a coal shovel. They parade in front of the tavern (a customer can be seen throwing up through the window) while a group of crippled beggars, legless and deformed, dance a pitiful and parodic round behind them.[1]

On a street corner behind the beggars, another masquerade relates the tale of Orson and Valentine. The subject is borrowed from a French romance published in 1489. Two little boys, the tale relates, were abandoned in the woods, and after various adventures, one of them wound up in the court of King Pippin and became the knight Sir Valentine while the other found his way into a bear's den. The bear brought the child up in a fatherly fashion according to his lights, and Orson became a wild man, a man of the woods. He frequently appears in medieval imagery, quite independently from this story, and the *Wilden Mann* is a regular figure of German carnivals (a reminiscence of the Greek Dionysus?) even today. Each year, in the Basel carnival, he can be seen descending the Rhine on a raft. The scene in the painting represents the moment when Valentine, having just captured his hirsute twin, is presenting him to the royal court. Orson, after that, good-naturedly allows himself to be tamed and becomes the servant and faithful companion of his knightly brother. Around the two groups masks can be seen collecting donations (in the same pear-shaped money boxes seen earlier in a print). Behind them, at the end of the street, a group has gathered around a bonfire on which Winter is being burned in effigy.

On the other side of the square, people are leaving church. Those who have chairs take them back home with them. The devout, dressed in black, give alms to

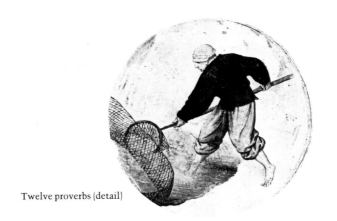

Twelve proverbs (detail)

beggars and cripples. But this part of the original painting, as the study of a copy by Peter Brueghel the Younger reveals, has been drastically overpainted in several places. The sheet lying on the ground on the lower right-hand corner originally covered the legs of an emaciated man lying flat on his back, exhibiting his huge, bloated belly. Farther up, and beyond the edge of the original work in its present state, stands a man with a severely deformed arm. The little cart pulled by the woman near the center of the painting originally contained not fish and a basket, but the impotent body of an old woman. Finally, at the foot of the round table beside the church door, one can still make out the darker area where Bruegel had painted three crippled children lying on the ground.[2]

Let us now draw closer to the vortex of the painting. On its outer edge, to the right, is the fishmonger's stall (fish being a characteristic Lenten food); to the left, totally absorbed in her task, is the waffle maker (then as today, an inexpensive festive food), cooking her wares on a fire of twigs. The position of her body and her concentration on her work provide a fine instance of the importance Bruegel always gave to characteristic gestures and attitudes of the human body at work.

And finally, at the very center of this anarchic round, we come to a small zone of peace. To the left, a couple is walking away both from the spectator and from all the noisy celebration. The man is guiding his wife with a protective gesture. And one may wonder: Should they be regarded as the antithesis of all the rest? Have these people found wisdom and inner peace? Perhaps not, for they are following a Fool bearing a torch while the woman carries a lantern hanging from her belt but fails to use it. This suggests that we may be looking at yet another allusion to the theme of universal madness that Erasmus, some forty years earlier, had presented as the sole guide and mistress of mankind. Beside them, however, is a well, and a woman is drinking from the bucket she has drawn up. One might fail to notice her, but she could well be the utterly unspectacular figure of wisdom that Bruegel presents in contrast with the "madness" he chose for his theme. The woman could be said to be drinking

---

[1] Bruegel has treated this subject separately in a small painting now in the Louvre.

[2] A study of the copy of this painting by Peter Brueghel the Younger was published by Jacquelin Folie in completing the posthumous publication of Georges Marlier's book *Pieter Brueghel le Jeune*.

at the spring (or well) of Nature and of Scripture, seeking God and the meaning of things in inner silence and reflectiveness. One should bear in mind that, already in the fourteenth century, a serious form of mystical thought had succeeded in touching a broad popular audience in the German-speaking countries. This influence extended through Alsace and the German principalities all the way to the Netherlands. This mystical thought made its influence felt in various social classes and more particularly among the craftsmen who, while they were not learned men, were inclined to meditate on all manner of things. In the light of what has already been said concerning his treatment of the seven deadly sins and the virtues, we may suppose that Bruegel, under the pretext of dealing with an entertaining subject, lent his painting a quasi-symphonic complexity and revealed, in a more ambitious and elaborate form, his thoughts on the "madness" that can be seen raging on either side of the painting.

Crazy Griet (*Dulle Griet*) (1562?) is the title van Mander uses to designate one of Bruegel's more difficult works. The title does not seem to be of any real help when it come to understanding what the work is about. The various interpretations that have so far been put forward strike me as somewhat unfounded and I am not absolutely sure my own attempts will do much to improve the situation. But I shall give it a try nonetheless.

The painting is once more an allegory in the style of the series of prints devoted to the seven deadly sins. Griet, the central figure, has a number of points in common with the personification of *Wrath* in that series: the armor, the iron glove, the helmet, and the sword, but also the swift, aggressive stride. Under her left arm she carries various precious objects, along with a jug and a skillet. The mouth of Hell gapes nearby, and devils can be seen swarming all over the place. On a bridge behind Griet a troop of women have managed to throw a small band of monsters to the ground and are busily trussing them like chickens (see number 40 in the list of Flemish proverbs at the end of this chapter) while others beat off a group of assailants, some of which are human. But while they are busied in this way, a grim contingent of men in armor is shown wading upstream toward the bridge in a bid to outflank them. This peculiar painting might conceivably justify the arguments of those who are intent on discovering a political allegory in Bruegel's work. It could be read as an "Allegory of Spain" as seen through Flemish eyes: Bruegel's country had suffered from the fierce depredation of Spanish troops, from the manifestations of the Spanish king's *folie religieuse,* and it had even felt itself threatened with the Inquisition—an institution that was inclined to discover devils everywhere and was itself quite capable of acts of diabolical cruelty.

But now let's carry things a bit further: B. Claessens and J. Rousseau (in *Notre Bruegel*) have this to say about the circumstances in which the "Landjuweel" (the national competition of the Chambers of Rhetoric) was held in 1561: "In Antwerp the 'Landjuweel' was the occasion of celebrations that lasted a full month. Two thousand rhetoricians took part in it. It was also the occasion of countless barbs against the régime. Burgomaster An-

toine van Straalen was jailed and the freedom and audacity displayed, both in speech and in writing, during these festivities ultimately cost him his life." One may recall that both Bruegel's employer Jerome Cock and his friend Franckert were members of a Chamber of Rhetoric known as the Stock-flower. Bruegel himself must have been kept posted on all these events from day to day. The very next year, in 1562 (once more according to Claessens and Rousseau), "Christophe Plantin was forced to leave Antwerp in order to escape proceedings for heresy."[3] And that same year, I suggest, Bruegel, who had been deeply impressed by recent events, painted an "Allegory of Spain" in which this powerful master is portrayed as a crazy shrew. After this he quite suddenly left Antwerp and headed for Amsterdam. One might well wonder what led Bruegel to undertake this trip. Could it have been a fear of reprisals? Finally, in 1563, Bruegel left Antwerp for good and settled in Brussels. Van Mander says it was at the request of his future mother-in-law, but there could have been other reasons, too. One last point concerns the title. I have said that it could not help us to understand the painting—but the reverse may be true: The interpretation I have proposed for the painting may possibly throw some light on the title. Let us suppose now that Bruegel did in fact refer to the painting in an informal and familiar way as *Dulle Griet. Griet,* in Flemish, is a diminutive of Margaret—and Margaret (Marguerite) was the name of the Duchess of Parma, the regent who was applying Philip II's grim policies in Flanders and who was probably held responsible for them by some people, including Bruegel himself. *Dulle Griet* would, in this case, turn out to be *Mad Meg*—the regent herself.

Now, if we take a pencil and connect the dots of all these little facts or suppositions in the right order, we shall discover a picture. The existence of other pictures, however, though they that may not show the pleasing coherence of the hypothesis ventured above, may be regarded as quite as likely.

In any event, this is the painting in which Bruegel comes closest to Hieronymus Bosch both in the intensity of his anguish and in the horror of his diabolical world. One does still come across a few quaint, round-eyed little devils, but the painting as a whole conveys a sense of distress, which could imply that Bruegel, despite his sturdy moral constitution, had been shaken by some significant event at the time that he painted it.

During that same time (1562–63), he also produced *The Triumph of Death.* It is the last, and possibly the most impressive, of Bruegel's allegorical works. The theme is entirely in the medieval tradition, whether French (the "Danse Macabre" in the Cemetery of the Innocents), German (Hans Holbein and Niklaus Manuel Deutsch both painted a "Totentanz"), or Italian. The Italian tradition appears to have given preference to "The Triumph of Death" (as in the fresco in the Palazzo Sclafani in Palermo).

Bruegel went a step further than all of these, making

---

[3] Pantin, a friend of Ortels and one of the great printers of the Renaissance, sought refuge in Paris.

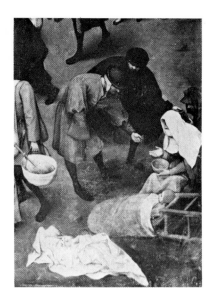

Peter Bruegel the Elder: the
Battle of Carnival and Lent
Detail.

Peter Bruegel the Younger:
copy of same before the
original was overpainted.

a synthesis of both subjects and bringing them together in what German writers refer to as a *Weltlandschaft*, a landscape embracing an entire world.

In this painting the central allegorical figure, Death himself in the guise of one of the horsemen of the Apocalypse, appears at the intersection of two diagonal lines that determine the structure of the entire work. He is shown waving his scythe, but the gesture is merely symbolic since the real task is already being accomplished by an army of skeletons standing on either hand. Behind the figure of Death there appears a mouth of Hell mounted on wheels, exactly in the design of those used on the stage in medieval religious mysteries. In the present case it looks something like a war machine, belching fire and smoke, and a few devils can be seen looking out. But for the moment the stage belongs to Death. The devils will have to wait their turn.

Dividing the painting into two equal parts horizontally, one finds that the lower half is reserved to scenes illustrating the familiar statement about the equalizing power of death. Skeletons are seen carrying off (from left to right) an emperor, a prelate, a mother and her baby child, a knight, a lansquenet, some fine court ladies, and a couple of lovers absorbed in a duet. Other figures can be seen higher up in the general stampede, rushing to escape the fatal scythe and falling into the nets of death. The entire lower half of the painting is treated pretty much in the idiom of tapestry, and almost without perspective.

The upper half, on the other hand, unfolds a broad panoramic view of devastation. Even to a modern spectator who has seen many such scenes on television and in picture magazines, the vision is impressive. Taking his departure from a subject that had become conventional, allegorical, and entirely formalized, Bruegel managed to express his perception of the challenge proposed by the utter negation of all life and all values by death. The power of death disrupts all things; the constructions of political power collapse, and the good earth itself is turned to desert under the effect of its devastating fire. "And now, what are we going to do?" This is a question that is felt with even more acuity in our own age than it was in the sixteenth century; there was still a dominant religious vision then that postulated the existence of a beyond in which all contradictions would ultimately be resolved. But Bruegel, among all the artists of his day, is the least willing to resign himself to awaiting a resolution that would only come after death.

In this painting he allows the allegorical figure of Death to formulate the most radically negative utterance he can manage and to confront the viewer with the ultimate derision of his question: "Here's what I am capable of doing. What about you?" Bruegel attends to the question with earnest attention. He pauses to consider. Then, once his thoughts have ripened, he begins to paint. One might say that each one of his paintings, until the very end, was like a new and, each time, provisional answer to this fundamental question.

43

30. Numbers refer to the proverbs listed below.

List of the Main Proverbs

1. The broom is before the door (the masters are away)
2. Married under the broom (an unmarried couple)
3. To look through one's fingers (to allow people to gossip)
4. To stand there with one's clogs on (to wait in vain)
5. Griddle cakes grow on the roof (they have things in abundance)
6. To shoot one arrow after another (one's efforts are unrewarded)
7. The hogs are in the corn (everything is going wrong)
8. His ass is on fire (he is in a hurry)
9. He plays (music) in the stocks (he does not realize he is ridiculous)
10. The knife is hanging (a sign of defiance, a challenge)
11. Fools get the best cards
12. To hold one another by the nose (to dislike one another)
13. He shits on the world (he cares for nothing)
14. The dice have been thrown
15. There's a hole in the roof (he has a screw loose)
16. He has thick skin behind the ears (he is a rogue, a swindler)
17. To piss at the moon (to strive after something impossible)
18. There are slates on the roof (walls have ears)
19. Two fools under the same bonnet
20. He shaves the fool without soap (he is making fun of him)
21. Topsy-turvy world
22. All depends on how the cards fall
23. To see through the scissors' eyes (to make a profit)
24. To keep a nest egg
25. To tie each herring by its own gills (each man must pay for himself)
26. To sit down between two chairs with one's bum in the ashes
27. Let the dog in, he'll go to the cupboard (give him an inch, and he'll take a yard)
28. The shears are hanging out front (the customer is sure to be fleeced)
29. He is always gnawing at the same bone
30. The pulse taker (the womanizer)
31. To carry the news of the day in a basket (to reveal what should be kept secret)
32. To light a candle to the Devil
33. To tell one's sins to the Devil
34. He carries fire in one hand and water in the other (he is not to be trusted)
35. The sow unstops the barrel (the innkeeper is not minding his business)
36. Armed to the teeth
37. A man in armor bells the cat (weapons make even cowards brave)
38. One loads the distaff, the other spins (they gossip)
39. She wraps her husband in a blue cloak (she is unfaithful)
40. She could tie the devil to a cushion (a woman could outsmart the Devil)
41. To beat one's head against the wall
42. One man shears the sheep, another the pig (one is wealthy, the other poor)
43. Meek as a lamb
44. He turns his coat with the wind
45. He throws feathers to the wind
46. Fear makes old people run
47. When the blind lead the blind, both fall into the ditch
48. No one weaves a web so fine that the sun does not show it

49. To sail before the wind
50. To shit beneath the gallows (a gesture of defiance)
51. To stand gaping at the stork
52. To kill two flies at one blow (two birds with one stone)
53. If the house burns down, he warms himself by the embers (he sees the best in all things)
54. To drag a stump behind one
55. Horse droppings are not figs
56. Why do geese walk barefoot? (There is a reason for all things)
57. To fall off the ox and onto the donkey (to change subjects)
58. To kiss the ring (to submit)
59. To rub ones bum against the door (one couldn't care less)
60. Two men shit through the same hole (they make a virtue of necessity)
61. To throw one's money onto water (out the window)
62. To hang one's tunic on the gate (to defrock or to change professions)
63. To watch the bears dancing (to starve)
64. To swim against the tide
65. To catch eels by the tail
66. The jug is brought to the well so often that it finally breaks
67. You can cut fine straps out of other people's leather (to be generous with other people's property)
68. To fish behind other people's nets (to be content with leftovers)
69. Big fish eat the smaller ones
70. To be furious because the sun shines in the water (to be envious)
71. Fox and crane make a pair
72. It is healthy to piss on the fire
73. To know how to catch fish with one's hands (to be clever in business)
74. To sit on burning embers
75. To take the chicken's egg and lose that of the goose (to lose a big advantage for a small one)
76. To hang between heaven and earth
77. To fall and break the basket (to ruin one's chances)
78. You bleed the pig through the belly
79. Two dogs can't agree on a bone
80. To give our Lord a beard of tow (to think one is getting away with something)
81. To sit in the light
82. He fills the well after the calf has been drowned
83. To throw roses to the swine
84. To have the world dancing on one's thumb
85. To draw the blanket to one
86. To yawn before the oven (to be good for nothing)
87. One must know how to stoop if one wishes to get ahead in the world
88. To poke sticks into other people's wheels (to hamper their undertakings)
89. When you let the gruel fall, you can't pick it all up
90. His hands are tied
91. He can't manage from one bread to the next (he can't make both ends meet)
92. To chose the small axe (to be a lazy worker)

31. THE FLEMISH PROVERBS *Detail of upper right-hand side of the painting (about half the size of the original).*

32. THE FLEMISH PROVERBS *(1559) Oil on wood panel, 118 × 163 cm.*

33. CHILDREN'S GAMES *(1560) Oil on wood panel, 118 × 161 cm.*

34.

35.

34–37. CHILDREN'S GAMES *Details.*

36.

37.

38. THE BATTLE OF CARNIVAL AND LENT *Detail: the fishmonger.*

39. THE BATTLE OF CARNIVAL AND LENT *(1559) Oil on wood panel 118 × 164.5 cm.*

40. THE BATTLE OF CARNIVAL AND LENT *Detail: The Masquerade of Orson and Valentine.*

42. THE WEDDING OF MOPSUS AND NISA *(after 1556) Ink drawing on wood, 26.6 × 41.6 cm.*

41. THE MASQUERADE OF ORSON AND VALENTINE *(1566) Woodcut, 27.5 × 41 cm (only woodcut known to be have made from a work by Bruegel).*

43. THE BATTLE OF CARNIVAL AND LENT *Detail: The Wedding of Mopsus and Nisa.*

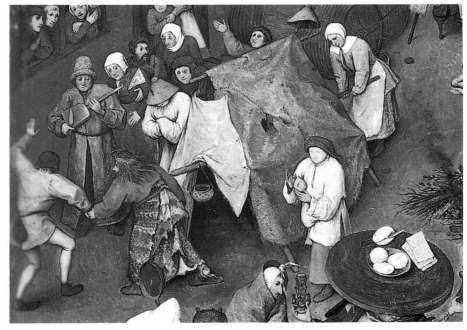

44. CRAZY GRIET (DULLE GRIET) *Detail: Griet*

45. CRAZY GRIET (DULLE GRIET) *or* MAD MEG *(1562?) Oil on wood panel, 115 × 161 cm.*

46. CRAZY GRIET (DULLE GRIET) *Detail.*

47. CRAZY GRIET (DULLE GRIET) *Detail.*

48. THE TRIUMPH OF DEATH *Detail: a prelate seized by death.*

49. THE TRIUMPH OF DEATH *(1562–1563) Oil on wood panel, 117 × 162 cm.*

50. **THE TRIUMPH OF DEATH** *Detail: landscape in the upper half of the painting.*

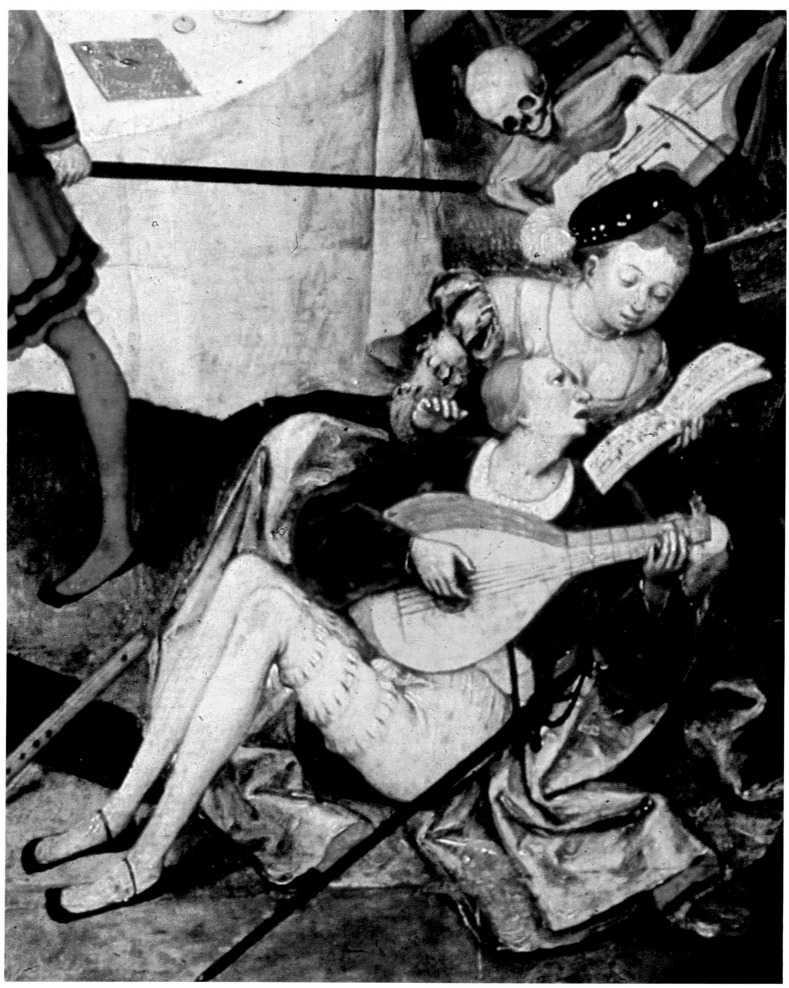

51. THE TRIUMPH OF DEATH *Detail: musicians.*

52. THE TRIUMPH OF DEATH *Detail.*

53. THE TRIUMPH OF DEATH *Detail: dead woman and child.*

54. THE TRIUMPH OF DEATH *Detail: the crowd and the skeleton army.*

55. THE TRIUMPH OF DEATH *Detail.*

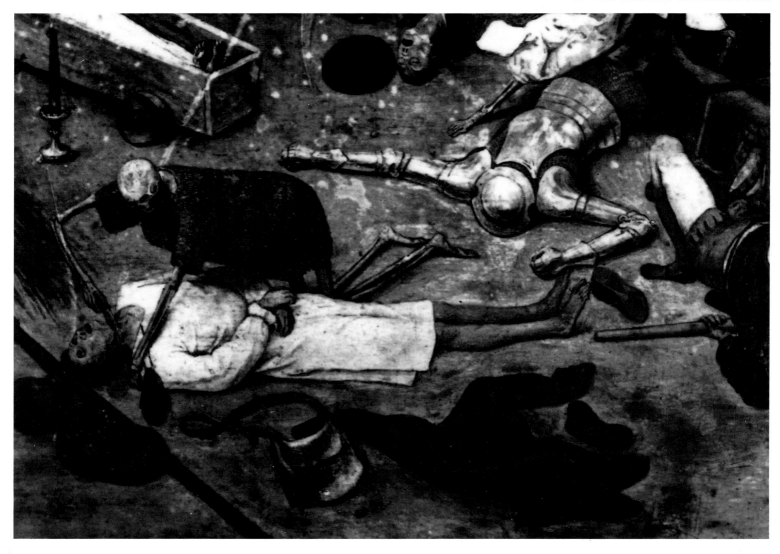

III. – In The Cleft

Epiphany (about 1556)

A religious painting can just as well be the product of a dogmatic rule or an entirely personal reflection. In either case it should be viewed as an attempt to deal with the question that, in Bruegel's work, found its ultimate expression in *The Triumph of Death*: "What is the significance of the world and of our own existence?" One does not need to be faced with such an overwhelming "epiphany of the negative"[1] in order to ask oneself this question. The very fact that we live can be quite as astonishing to some as the fact that we die, and Bruegel, in his earliest works, does indeed seem to have been amazed by the inexhaustible splendor of the world, just as he would later be troubled by the destructive power of all that is negative in human experience.

The contradiction arising out of this twofold aspect of reality cries out for a solution, and Bruegel, in his own idiosyncratic way, gave the matter his fullest attention, expressing his views in the common language afforded by the established beliefs of the day. Any reflection of this kind must inevitably make use of an existing body of symbols if it is to develop at all, but to those who look beyond the obvious charm of his art and the breathtaking expanses of his landscapes and start examining his underlying conceptions, the fundamental interest of Bruegel's work in this domain resides in the way he was constantly overstepping the fixed boundaries of religious language itself.

Before his time, the medieval worldview had been dependent on a body of revealed truths supplemented by a variety of fantasies—some of them threatening, some serene. After his death, the violent events stirred up by the Reformation gradually subsided. In Catholic countries, new rules were set down by the Counter-Reformation. The new policy was intended to keep a tight rein on everything that touched upon religious doctrine, particularly in the realm of the arts. As a result of this policy, all religious paintings were subject to highly formal regulations that practically denied the artist any opportunity of working out his own ideas and expressing his own perception of things. While this policy obviously did not prevent the tremendous flowering of the seventeenth and eighteenth centuries, it would ultimately extenuate all real creativity in the religious realm. Artists, reduced to the role of executants and apologists of notions they had not elaborated themselves, were led to turn to the heritage of the Italian Renaissance for guidance and inspiration; and the heritage itself, in the process, was reduced to a set of predictable conventions that gradually degenerated until nothing but the academic model remained. Since artists no longer had anything say to about content, they could do little more than strive after various kinds of formal refinements. Only two centuries later, the decline of religious art was consummated. Of course, numerous factors intervened and the strict controls enforced by the Counter-Reformation were only partly to blame.

Somehow, between these two masses—between the medieval dream or fantasy on the one hand and the well-regulated propaganda on the other—Bruegel managed to drive his spiritual and esthetic roots into one of those deep and fertile spiritual clefts or faults that occasionally open up in the uniform desert of official certainties and allow some authentic notions to unfold. The people Bruegel was in touch with daily during his years in Antwerp included a good number of tolerant and learned men: geographers, botanists, and doctors of medicine who made man and the world the object of their study and who constantly strove to understand the religious faith they had inherited and that still afforded them the only cosmology and the only coherent representation of man's fate they could conceive. It was for men such as these—for their eyes, at least, and for their minds—that Bruegel undertook to paint his religious works.

Even before painting *The Triumph of Death*, Bruegel had produced a smaller and much more intimate work that might be regarded as an epigraph to what was yet to come. It is a drawing, done in the manner of a grisaille, whose subject is *The Resurrection of Christ* (1562), and looking at it today, one may perceive it as an anticipatory dream in which the still implicit colors have yet to be touched by the light or the fire of day.

The Resurrection of Christ is the only truly triumphant work in Bruegel's entire production. *The Adoration of the Magi* (1564) might justifiably have been handled in this spirit, yet Bruegel chose a different approach. It is all the more striking then that he should have failed to render the Resurrection in the vigorous range of colors that are so well suited to the subject, for here was a theme that clearly offered the most daring and radical negation of death one could imagine. Yet while he availed himself of the full range of color and its strong emotional realism to formulate the challenge of death, Bruegel chose to express the triumphant negation of negation in singularly muted tones. He undoubtedly believed in the risen Christ. Such matters were not open to doubt in his day: Not

---

[1] "Epiphany" means the unveiling of a supernatural presence. Thus the feast of the Epiphany recalls the recognition, by the Magi, of the divinity incarnate in an infant child. The "negative" referred to here is death itself, considered as a force of dissolution. In this sense *The Triumph of Death* can be regarded as an "epiphany of the negative."

only were they unacceptable, they were practically unthinkable. But the Resurrection, in his sight, was still no more than a premise and a pledge; no matter how firm his faith may have been on this point, a blatantly triumphant rendering would have struck him as premature in view of the grim evidence of death and suffering that still held (hold) the upper hand.

The painting offers a narrative synthesis of three distinct moments of the gospel story: 1) As Christ emerges from the tomb, the guards, set there to ensure that the body is not removed, go on sleeping; 2) the guards awaken to discover that the heavy stone has been rolled aside and that the tomb is empty; 3) the women come to the tomb at dawn to wash the body, and an angel is waiting to tell them that Christ is risen. The drawing, though badly deteriorated (a fine print of the same subject also exists) is nonetheless supremely eloquent, particularly in the attitude of the two soldiers pointing down into the bottomless gullet of the grave from which the luminous apparition has just emerged.

The coherence of the first sequence of religious works will no doubt become more apparent if we try to view it as a structured whole that tentatively emerges, after the fashion of a musical figure, out of the preceding motive, then gradually fleshes itself out, and gains in assurance until it proclaims its message in a strongly colored and indeed lyrical form of realism. This new motive, as we shall see, only gradually asserts itself, gaining in volume and intensity until the obsessional trumpet calls and lugubrious drumrolls of the funeral march are at last quite eclipsed and the sequence (or movement) closes in a first vision of serenity. When Bruegel painted *The Resurrection* and *The Triumph of Death* in 1562, he also dealt with *The Fall of the Rebel Angels* and *The Death of Saul*—both of them mythic figures of failure and collapse within the supernatural realm—within the realm, in other words, in which a *meaning* as a response to the enigma of death, is expected to appear. In 1563 Bruegel also produced both versions of the *Tower of Babel* as well as *The Flight into Egypt*. In 1564, finally, he painted nothing but religious subjects: *The Adoration of the Magi*, *The Way to Calvary*, and *The Death of the Virgin*. These paintings represent a first coherent group of such works and a first high point in the artist's career, though Bruegel, who was always maturing his understanding and broadening his outlook, never ceased moving on to higher accomplishments.

The Fall of the Rebel Angels is an entirely traditional subject, and Bruegel handles it in a seemingly Gothic idiom. The subject itself is not really a biblical one, being derived from a parallel tradition according to which a number of angels (for reasons that vary from one tale to the next) rebelled against their creator. This led to a battle at the end of which the rebels were defeated and cast down into the abyss. Bruegel approached the subject in his own adaptation of the idiom of Hieronymus Bosch. But there is a new and indeed "modern" aspect to his treatment of the subject, and it is apparent in the unusual viewpoint he chose. Starting at the top of the picture in a remote and luminous region of heaven, the rout of the rebel angels (who can be seen gradually turning into monsters) has become a free-fall into the void. Their mass bears down upon the viewer like a threatening avalanche. Should this unusual choice of a point of view be regarded as a merely formal solution? That seems most unlikely. More plausibly, Bruegel found this means of involving the spectator in the cosmic disaster. The angels in Bruegel's representation are archaic and impersonal figures, while the devils—those, at least, who still have human faces—exude a horrified anguish. The nature of their emotion will no doubt seem more intelligible to us if we compare it to the intimate anguish of such familiar figures as the vampire, the werewolf, Jekyll-Hyde, or even the "living dead." All these suffer the condition of one who, like the equally pathetic "Elephant Man," has become a monster in spite of himself.

This painting assumes the role, in Bruegel's work, of an "original fall"—a mythic image accounting for the existence of evil and of death. But we have already been led to assume that, in Bruegel's view, monsters and devils are to be regarded as didactic figures of all human obsessions, vices, and follies. Bruegel, from the very outset, tends to remove evil from the supernatural realm and to relocate it in the psychological realm (one may be reminded of the ironical "shindies and ghostly apparitions" mentioned by van Mander, which clearly signify Bruegel's down-to-earth skepticism). In this way he offers a first intuitive formulation of a psychological notion that has become entirely familiar today, and *The Fall of the Rebel Angels*, taken as symbol of some original disaster might, in more modern terms, be regarded as a fatal fall *into* the unconscious. But then again, if we approach it from a different angle, it might equally well be taken as a figure of the fall of society as a whole away from the orderly spiritual representations of the medieval tradition and its descent into the chaos of cultural incoherence.

The Death of Saul is one of Bruegel's smaller works (33.5 × 55 cm), and it is painted in the style of a miniature. Bruegel's mother-in-law, Mayken Coeck (née Verhulst-Bessemers in the city of Malines) was reputed in her day as a miniaturist, and it may well be that she initiated her future son-in-law into this technique when he was a young apprentice to her husband, living in the comfortable and cultivated environment of their home. The painting represents a fine and varied landscape in which two armies, bristling with lances, can be seen engaged in combat. On closer scrutiny Saul can be made out standing to the left, away from the battle. He is about to throw himself on the sword. Bruegel gives the reference to the biblical text beside his signature: I Samuel, chapter 31.[2]

[2] The first book of Samuel, one of the first historical books in the Bible in which individual psychology plays any significant role, relates the life of Saul, the first king of Israel, and his replacement by David, designated by the prophet Samuel at a time when Saul was still reigning. Saul is not apprised of this, however, and David is brought into his retinue as a musician. It is David's task to appease the wild fits of terror that periodically overwhelm the king. David gradually draws attention to himself (his battle against Goliath), and Saul feels increasingly jealous, so much so, in fact, that he at one point attempts to pin him to the wall with his lance. David finds refuge with the

The event has a tragic quality, and its treatment might even remind one of the last scenes of *Macbeth*—but Bruegel's choice of subject does not allow for any simple explanation. Saul's failure, as it happens, opened the way to David's accession to the throne, and David, of course, is the archetypal monarch of the Old Testament. In the Psalms, of which he is presumed to be the author, David is presented as the embodiment of the Righteous Man, exposed to Saul's insane hostility, who ultimately gets his due and achieves the fine fulfillment of kingship. The painting does not necessarily refer directly to events then taking place in the Netherlands, but it may be assumed to express considerations arising out of the religious persecutions, which at the time afflicted a good number of sincere and tolerant men—some of whom were Bruegel's friends. In this view it may have expressed the hope that a period of fulfillment and serenity would eventually come.

The Tower of Babel exists in two versions, one large (114 × 155 cm) and one small (60 × 74.5 cm). It has been noted that the tower, in both of these, incorporates reminiscences of the Roman Coliseum, which Bruegel must have seen during his stay in Rome. The smaller tower is a splendid building that pierces the clouds like some man-made mountain peak. The larger painting includes a scene in the foreground in which a monarch, surrounded by his retinue, is shown visiting his stone cutters. The tower is in the process of being built around a large, natural rock formation that dominates the city and that the workers are gradually covering with masonry. The story of Genesis (chapter 11) that Bruegel illustrates has a true popular flavor and reflects the awed feelings of the 27,290 Jews condemned to exile in 732 B.C., when they first arrived in the great city of Babylon and discovered the imposing mass of the ziggurats that then dominated that imperial city.[3]

Two monkeys (1562)

This biblical tale that, like the fall of the rebel angels, touches upon yet another story of failure and disaster, lends itself perfectly to this grand treatment in a miniaturist's idiom. Bruegel's vision gives the subject an extraordinary breadth and includes a wealth of technical details rendered with encyclopedic precision. Here again the painting may express implicit criticism of the vaulting ambitions of the new monarchs who were then ruthlessly expanding and consolidating their kingdoms.

The Adoration of the Magi illustrates a New Testament narrative that is also marked by a popular flavor.[4] The staging of the scene is the usual one: The child is presented on his mother's lap; two of the wise men (who, according to tradition, were kings) are shown kneeling before the child to offer him their precious gifts; the third awaits his turn. Yet the painting is a surprising innovation in Bruegel's work so far, and it remains something unique in the history of western religious art.

What appears new here when we compare it to Bruegel's earlier work is the fact that the bodies, which in former paintings were squat and shapeless, are treated here in a monumental style, whereas the faces are more elaborately individualized and suggestive of strong and colorful characters. This is no doubt derived from a lesson that Bruegel must have learned in Italy, but which, as usual, he chose to apply in his own way. For while the overall composition is Italian enough, the characters are quite unlike the idealized and conventional figures, whether sentimental (Raphael) or Promethean (Michelangelo), that are so typical of Italian art. None of the players in this scene is really portrayed in the way convention demands. The Virgin for instance, is a real woman, endowed with a strong sensuality. She is unique in Bruegel's work as a whole (for the artist, as a rule, is not much concerned

Philistines, who are neighbors and enemies of his own people. Meanwhile, things take a turn for the worse for Saul. Samuel, who had always counseled him until then, dies; the Philistines start warlike movements. What is Saul to do? He turns to various oracles in search of reassurance, but none of them is willing to speak, so he decides to consult a necromancer, a woman who calls up the spirits of the dead. He asks her to call up Samuel. The ensuing scene has an undeniable grandeur. Samuel does indeed appear to foretell Saul's defeat, his death and the death of his sons, and the kingship given to David. The next day the battle of Gilboa ends in the rout of Saul's army. His sons are killed, and Saul himself wants to die. His squire, however, is too terrified to help him, so Saul throws himself on his own sword. Bruegel handles his subject without indulging in any of the Italian melodrama or rhetoric that would most likely have relegated the battle to the distant background.

[3] One can also imagine Jewish parents in Babylon trying to find a suitable answer to their children's questions: "At one time everyone spoke the same language. But as men moved east they found a broad plain and established themselves there. And they said to one another: 'Let us build a city and a tower whose top will pierce the heavens, that we may be remembered and not scattered over all the earth.' God descended one day to see the city and the tower, and he said to himself: 'Men are a single people and they speak a single language, and this is the beginning of their undertakings! Now nothing is impossible to them!' He therefore resolved to confound their languages, so that they might no longer understand one another. And once he had done this, they were no longer able to understand one another, and they were dispersed over the whole earth." After this, the parents might have

concluded, only the truncated monuments of the ziggurats remained as a vestige of this undertaking.

[4] Three Magi, astrologers or wise men ("from the East"), appeared one day at the court of King Herod. "Where is the king of the Jews who has just been born?" they asked. The king gathered all the wise men, who consulted the scriptures and informed Herod that the new king must have been born in Bethlehem. "Go then," Herod told the Magi, "and when you have found him, let me know, and I shall also go and pay homage." The Magi went and found Jesus to whom they offered gifts; then, "being warned in a dream," they returned home without calling on Herod. Joseph also received a warning and took the child and his mother to Egypt. As for Herod, he sent his soldiers to Bethlehem with orders to kill all children under the age of two. This provides the subject matter of three of Bruegel's paintings: *The Adoration of the Magi, The Flight into Egypt,* and *The Massacre of the Innocents.*

with feminine beauty) and unique in western art in general. Other artists have painted pretty Virgins, but none of these have the wordless power of full-blown femininity that is revealed as though by chance as the veil falls from her face. The muttered aside between Joseph and an unidentified supernumerary is also unusual. Instead of being engulfed, Italian fashion, in simpering or ecstatic contemplation, Joseph feels it is his duty to handle practical matters, even though respect for the royal visitors may authorize no more than a backward inclination of the head. As for the Magi, or at least the two of them who are bowing down (for the white-draped African king shows no more than a gentle and somewhat bemused profile), they present none of the usual traits one would expect to find in wise and noble ancients. The one to the left, in particular, has the bitter and tormented face of a man sorely tried by life. Even the halberdier standing behind the Virgin has the sincere and mildly perplexed expression of a mastiff who, placed before a kitten, cannot decide whether the creature should be protected or eaten. Such interpretations do not exclude others—they merely show something of the unusual zest and tang that Bruegel managed to inject into a subject as circumscribed by convention as this one is. Also, unlike his contemporary, Paolo Veronese, he did not have to submit the painting to the censorious eye of the Inquisition. The conclusion emerges quite gradually from Bruegel's treatment: The child that the Virgin holds on her lap and before whom the kings bow down is presented here to signify the key to the riddle, the answer ("the Word" in the language of the New Testament) by which the significance of human life is lit. But the faces surrounding him do not convey quite the same message as do the respectfully prostrated bodies. A lust shines out of them that bodes no good to the confident and smiling child. When one has seen this *Adoration*, the end of the story, the passion and the death, may appear entirely predictable.

A moment of respite comes nonetheless. *The Flight into Egypt* shows the object of this epiphany fading into a landscape of the kind Bruegel did so well, as vast as a world and as welcoming as the furthest horizons of a dream.

The next painting, *The Way to Calvary* (1564), is quite crucial in Bruegel's work. In it the Middle Ages and the Renaissance, the natural and the supernatural, the human crowd and the landscape are made to meet and merge. The subject is a public execution. Three men who have been sentenced to death are being led out of the town to one of those barren spots (Golgotha means "Place of the Skull") where the gallows, wheels, and crosses stand. Such executions were always a spectacle and an entertainment in the sixteenth century, and the population is shown following the condemned men, on foot or on horseback (the red-caped horsemen strung along the way are the militia). People can be seen moving along, swiftly or slowly, in an amusing variety of strides and attitudes. A patient art historian made a count of no fewer than five hundred human figures. A large circle has begun to form around the place of execution, and the audience is still growing. At the center of the painting,

lost in the crowd, Christ has just fallen under the weight of his cross. On the lower left some soldiers have been sent out to enlist the help of a passerby; the man they have laid hold of is Simon of Cyrene who, according to the gospel, carried the cross on the last lap to Calvary. Simon's wife, who seems familiar with the ways of the police, desperately clutches her man's arm, while other, more cautious bystanders have begun to scatter. Just ahead of Jesus, the two other condemned men, seated in a cart and livid with fear, are assisted by an anachronistic Christian monk who holds up the consoling cross in a gesture that could be either naïve or grimly ironical— after all, the people of Flanders had cause to fear that the Inquisition would be allowed to operate in their country. It's a windy day, and Bruegel manages to convey the fact by a few brilliant touches: the carefully observed attitudes of the ravens as they negotiate the eddies of the wind, the coats and banners flapping in the breeze, the nervous excitement of the horses and of the children. The weather is sunny over the town, but on the other side of the picture a threatening mass of clouds is being hustled along by the wind. The adults have come to witness an execution, drawn there by an unconscious and passive sadism. The children can be seen quarreling and teasing one another; they fight and play and enjoy skipping across the puddles left by yesterday's downpour. A peddler, seated in the foreground, turns his back to the viewer and watches the procession go by. Protestant polemicists at the time habitually referred to the Catholic Church as a peddler, because of the much criticized trade of indulgences. If the monk in the cart is indeed a figure of the Inquisition, then the peddler might in turn designate the Church, shown here as an indifferent witness to the crime. But then again, this one could conceivably be no more than a peddler.

A windmill that can be turned to catch every wind has been placed high on a rocky formation where it serves as the pivot of the whole gyratory movement. But it is in the foreground that we encounter one of Bruegel's most unexpected conceits; four figures, huddled together on a broad, flat rock seem to belong in a quite different world. They are Christ's mother, the apostle Saint John, and two other holy women, all of them overwhelmed with grief. Two traits distinguish them from the rest of the scene: the beautiful pathos of their emotions, and the fact that they are rendered in an idiom that harkens back to Rogier van der Weyden—long-limbed bodies, delicate hands, well-drawn faces, clothes disposed in ample Gothic drapery. Their inwardness bespeaks a quite different emotional range and seems quite beyond the countless little observations of daily life, so dear to Bruegel, that liven up the main scene. An intermediate group emerges from the crowd, looking up and sharing the transcendental sorrow of this sublime company. In the foreground, finally, Bruegel has placed some brambles, a thistle and a horse's skull . . .

Bruegel painted *The Death of the Virgin* (in 1564?) for his friend Ortels who subsequently (possibly in memory of Bruegel) had a print of it made for his friends. This painting is also a grisaille, and the death scene it depicts

56. THE RESURRECTION OF CHRIST *(1562) Grisaille on paper mounted on wood panel, 43 × 30.7 cm.*

57. THE RESURRECTION OF CHRIST *(1563) Copperplate engraving by Philippe Galle, 43.5 × 30 cm, published by J. Cock.*

is utterly serene. In this picture Mary, who brought God into the world, is cast neither as the *haute Déesse* (high Goddess) to whom François Villon addressed a supplication in his mother's name, nor as the Neoplatonic ikon that emerged in Italy with the Renaissance. Instead, she appears as the type of every human soul that has managed to establish a meaning and a goal for itself despite the baffling uncertainties of everyday life. This appears to be Bruegel's conclusion at the term of this first stage of his religious work. This painting offers an unemphatic response to the hyperbolic assertions of the grinning and triumphant skeleton. The outcome is paradoxical: His Virgin is indeed shown dying, yet, even so, she can be said to have overcome death, for she has, in the course of her life, managed to attain that central nucleus of the world and of her own self in which an answer and a

refutation may be found, even to such extreme derision. In this way the first motive of the funeral march can be heard once again in conclusion—but utterly changed. For now, in a humanist vision, it has taken on the form of a deep and gentle elegy.

Bruegel's reflections on this theme are certainly those of a believer, even though it is apparent too that he is paying closer attention to the symbolic import of his belief than to its strict dogmatic content. But if we can still understand his perception of things today, despite the fact that we are no longer steeped in the same vision ourselves, it must be because the question to which he strives to give an answer, the question raised at the outset by his allegorical skeleton with its absurd and disturbing scythe, is always with us and has, in one way or another, never ceased demanding a solution.

58. THE FALL OF THE REBEL ANGELS *(1562) Oil on wood panel, 117 × 162 cm.*

61. THE (LARGER) TOWER OF BABEL *Detail: the city and surrounding countryside.*

59. THE (SMALLER) TOWER OF BABEL *(1563) Oil on wood panel, 60 × 74.5 cm.*

60. THE (LARGER) TOWER OF BABEL *(1563) Oil on wood panel, 114 × 155 cm.*

62. THE (LARGER) TOWER OF BABEL *Detail: the tower.* *(See overleaf)*

64. **THE FLIGHT INTO EGYPT** *(1563) (Some reservations have been made as to its attribution to Peter Bruegel.) Oil on wood panel, 37.2 × 55.5 cm.*

65. **THE FLIGHT INTO EGYPT** *(about 1559) Ink drawing, 20.3 × 28.2 cm.*

63. **THE (LARGER) TOWER OF BABEL** *Detail: the port.*

66. **THE DEATH OF SAUL** *(1562) Oil on wood panel, 33.5 × 55 cm.*

67. THE DEATH OF THE VIRGIN *(1564)*
   Tempera on canvas, grisaille, 36 × 54.5 cm.

68. THE ADORATION OF THE MAGI *(1564)*
   Oil on wood panel, 108 × 83 cm.

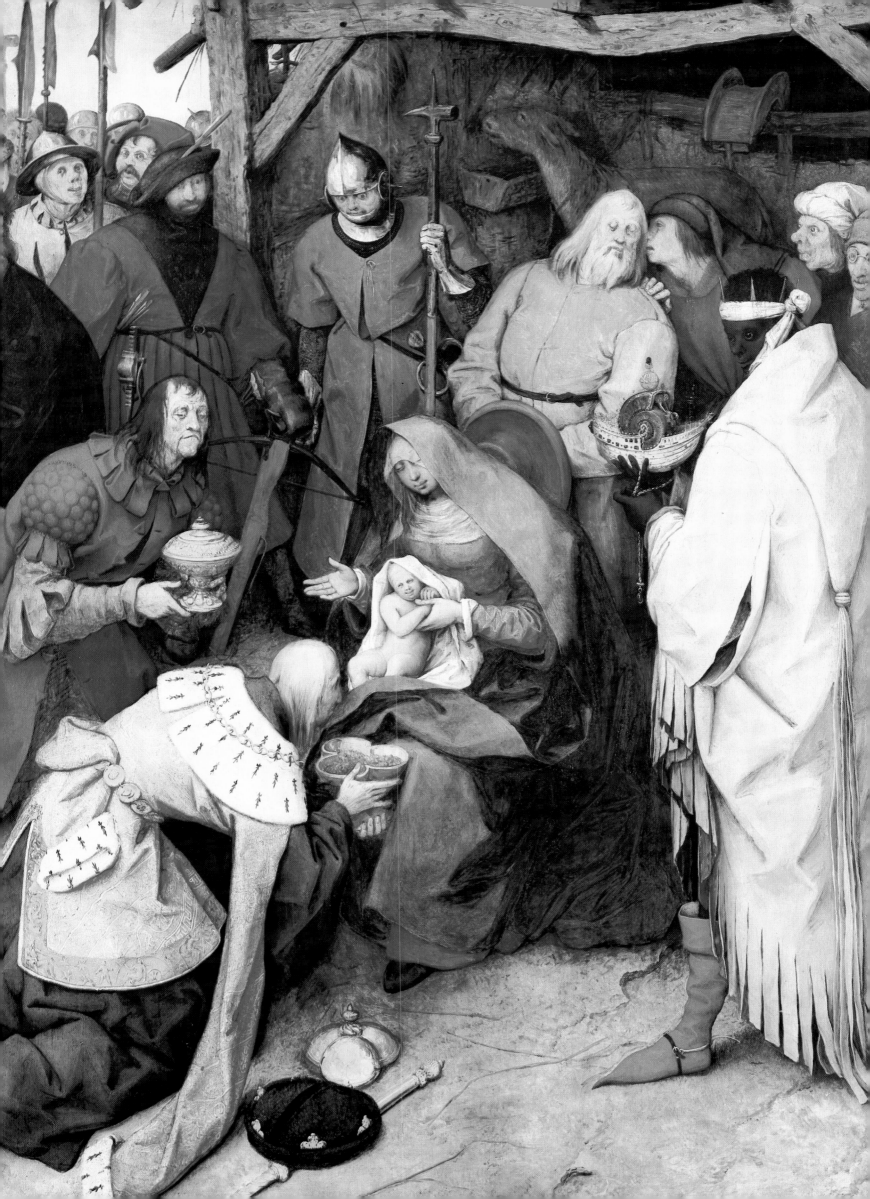

69. THE ADORATION OF THE MAGI *Detail: one of the kings (reproduced at approximately the original size).*

70. **THE ADORATION OF THE MAGI** *Detail: Saint Joseph (reproduced at approximately the original size).*

72. THE WAY TO CALVARY *Detail: the arrival of the militia.*

73. THE WAY TO CALVARY *Detail: Simon of Cyrene.*

71. **THE ADORATION OF THE MAGI** *Detail: Virgin and child (reproduced at approximately the original size).*

74. **THE WAY TO CALVARY** *(1564) Oil on wood panel, 124 × 170 cm. (See overleaf)*

75. **THE WAY TO CALVARY** *Detail: Jesus falls.*

76. **THE WAY TO CALVARY** *Detail: the crowd.*

77. THE WAY TO CALVARY *Detail: horsemen.*

78. THE WAY TO CALVARY *Detail: the cart with the condemned men.*

79. **THE WAY TO CALVARY** *Detail: The Virgin, St. John, and the Holy Women.*

80. THE WAY TO CALVARY *Detail: Golgotha.*

81. **THE WAY TO CALVARY** *Detail: the crowd going to Golgotha.*

IV. – The Imitation of Nature

It has long appeared obvious to a good number of people that the function of painting is simply (or primarily at least) to provide an accurate representation of the sights of the world.

Such a misconception stems in part, no doubt, from the countless statements of purpose issued by artists themselves ever since the Renaissance: "Paint nature . . . imitate nature . . . take nature as your guide. . . ." Such counsel is untiringly, one might even say obsessionally, repeated in essays and reflections on art. When Bruegel's friends or admirers want to praise him, they refer, among other things, to the ease with which he "follows nature" (van Mander, 1604) or "the ingenious and clever manner he had of imitating nature" (Ortels, 1573). One might thus be led to suppose that all the artists of this period, and Bruegel among them, assumed that their highest goal was, by virtuoso means, to render on paper, canvas, or wooden panel the true appearance of all things natural.

Such was the unthinking assumption of the nineteenth century that tended to consider artists of earlier times a bit awkward in this respect. But what did the notion of "painting, following, or imitating nature" actually imply in Bruegel's day? The question gains in importance as we turn to his landscapes. The key to the answer may well be found in the intentional stylistic contrast encountered in *The Way to Calvary*. What models did Renaissance painters have before their eyes? When the Italian painters undertook the great philosophical and esthetic mutation long before any other nation further to the north, they had before them the Byzantine model: The ikon and the set rules governing its figures had remained dominant in Italy until the thirteenth century; the Netherlands, on the other hand, had, until the fifteenth century, lived with the canons of the Gothic style, which had its own specific stylization and its particular form of expressionism. This was an art of the highest quality, and Bruegel, in his rendering of the group of saints, pays it a final homage and gives us a sampling of the work he might have done had he remained a Gothic artist. But the other aspect of the painting reveals what the "imitation of nature" meant to him.

The Gothic part refers to a representation of the world whose decline signifies the collapse of the medieval world view. In that time everything appeared motivated, or was at least required, to justify itself in reference to the supernatural. There was undoubtedly an art of profane entertainment, but not much of it has survived— probably for the same reason that has led to the disappearance of most of the carved wooden horses of the old merry-go-rounds. There was also an art designed to show off extreme wealth and lend its brilliance to the homes of the powerful. These were decorative arts, in fact, and

Skaters with bird trap (1565)

they have often survived to this day because of the precious materials of which they were made. But Bruegel, by his training, was heir to the great tradition of religious art—an art that followed rules derived from the cosmology of the theologians. Thus the basic model was not nature, but the spiritual patterns and religious precepts, together with the style elaborated by earlier masters to which the new generation no doubt felt itself entitled to bring refinements. Some of these refinements, like the unprecedented human pathos that appears in the work of a van der Weyden, could be quite radical. But this never prevented the model of art from remaining a predominantly theological one.

And why? Because the answer to the most fundamental and serious question touching upon the meaning of the world and of all human existence was to be sought after in the theological domain alone. It was only through the supernatural and its mediation, that some sort of coherence could appear in the confusion and disasters of earthly existence. Thus, for a man of the sixteenth century, "the imitation of nature" could represent an adventure without precedent and implied that the *meaning* of the world and of existence was thenceforth to be sought in a domain from which it had, until then, been excluded. The very notion of "natural cause" had a daring and innovative ring about it that we can hardly conceive of today, and it began to be distinctly articulated at about that time, for instance in the book, published in 1555 under the significant title *De Naturalium Causis*, by the Italian philosopher Pietro Pomponazzi. "Follow nature" was consequently the daring watchword of men who wished to enter upon a new way of thought and life without yet knowing where it would lead them.

One thing was certain, however: This new way was not intended to lead to the seclusion of some intellectual belvedere that would offer a panoramic view of the world as though it were a mere *spectacle*. These adventurers of the mind had embarked, rather, on a search for a more complete and complex answer to the question of *meaning* raised by the natural world and to the challenge that it represented for the human mind. Art, until then, had been engaged in signifying the supernatural (and invisible) world by means of figures drawn from the visible, precisely because it was assumed that the meaning of all things was concealed in the supra-sensible. But henceforth, these adventurous minds decided, one would have to turn one's attention to the visible and the tangible and, because its independent coherence was beginning to impress the more observant, to the *natural* rather than to the *supernatural* order. The coherence and intelligibility of nature was a constant surprise to the men of the Renaissance. All this led Bruegel to draw and paint nature. Others had ventured this way before him, but he followed and overtook them with an entirely innovative mastery; he observed nature not just as one might consider a field or a wood, but by approaching it as one might a door giving access to a realm whose very existence no one had anticipated until then. He had all at once been struck, in other words, by its inherent logic and its breathtaking grandeur. And so, when he drew his mountains, it was not just to give a topographical account of them, but to bear witness to the existence of a spiritual and geographical space into which he had gone striding with wide-open eyes. How many men had, just like Bruegel, crossed the Alps over the centuries? How many of these had been artists? And what sort of image had they born away with them? Ethnology, which is, all told, a fairly recent discipline, has allowed us to understand something of the way in which different cultures, faced with the same facts, perceive different meanings and even different physical appearances.

Bruegel, then, on his return from his journey, was not merely turning in a report. He was attempting to get the spectator involved in this adventure of nature—he wanted him to *see* what he himself had seen. But what had that been? One might say a substance: the world of the *object* (in opposition to the divine world of the *subject*); and a scope: its space beyond appeal, its time beyond return. This does not amount to a negation of the supernatural realm. Bruegel's age could not even have imagined such a possibility. Quite to the contrary, both terms continued to coexist side by side, but nature (despite countless philosophical difficulties) was beginning to take on the appearance of a realm singularly well suited to the fulfillment of mankind. In art, consequently, nature no longer served as a mere stage set on which a religious pageant, an episode in the drama of redemption, could unfold. The setting itself became an actor in the drama. This is seminally present in the travel drawings. When young Bruegel returned to Antwerp, all these things were still fermenting in his heart and had been tucked away in his folders; but then, surprisingly enough, he would, over the next ten years, only gradually approach this reality that he had, on first encounter, grasped with such unwavering acuity. Still, on second thought, it may not be quite that surprising after all. His return to Antwerp had brought him back to a quite different reality—that of the community in which he had grown up and to which he had returned, after a journey of several years, with an eye refreshed by distance. No matter that he returned full of all manner of sights and of the sheer immensity of space; his return reimmersed him in the deep and familiar opacity of society. And if he took ten years to rediscover his first, transparent intuition, it could be that this much

time was needed for him to build a suitable bridge between these two terms and bring them face-to-face.

Looking at the drawings done between 1552 and 1556 (there are twenty-five of them), one is immediately struck by the invariance of the subject matter despite the diversity of its representations: They all deal with the mountain and its huge mass, the bone structure of its rocks, the muscular anatomy of its flanks. Bruegel's journey led him down to Sicily and then back up through all of Italy with its splendid cities, its people, its landscapes, its monuments. His later work shows us, allusively, that he has perceived all this too, but meanwhile all he can manage to say is "mountain, mountain, mountain."

These drawings convey the strong impression of an *accurate* representation. That too is quite impressive. His mountains don't have the fanciful appearance encountered in the work of such entirely delightful predecessors as Joachim Patenier. One senses, looking at the latter's work, that his approach is that of a transcendental landscape gardener: "Just set that rock over there, beside the pond . . ." Bruegel, on the contrary, was attentive to the immanent logic of geology and of erosion. Most of the time he drew what he had seen—what he had known *how* to see. Yet he could not have made us see this so distinctly if he had failed to add, to the existing articulation of the landscape, a secondary articulation provided by the narrative lines of force that appeared as he set the scene to paper. Bruegel systematized the configuration of the Alps in order to allow us to grasp their true appearance, and in doing so his rendering departs from what a tracing done with a camera lucida might have revealed. It is apparent in these drawings that he already knew how to make use of the flexible interplay of diagonal lines to lead the spectator off into the depth of the landscape. He was already a tremendous storyteller who knew how to draw his viewer after him through the plain, up along the mountain slopes, and right up to the far-off crests that remain constantly shrouded in the clouds of an unresolved question.

The journey yielded drawings that were all completed over a five-year period, the last of them in 1556. Another sequence of signed drawings, dated between 1560 and 1562, was also widely attributed to Bruegel until fairly recently. When I wrote the French version of this book I accepted the verdict of the experts, noting only that the treatment of the landscape was surprisingly different from all the rest of Bruegel's production: "The Alps of the first large drawings have turned into bizarre and picturesque rock formations, bordering a river on which idyllic little boats sail across waters untouched by any passion. Or again they are shown capped by tumbledown little castles, the meeting place of lovers and of owls among the brambles. The rolling landscape is dotted with cozy little farmhouses or villages nestled under the thick down of the trees." A more recent appraisal (by Hans Mielke) has, to my satisfaction, removed these drawings from the Bruegel catalogue and reattributed them to Jacques Savery.

In 1565 Bruegel delivered a series of landscape paintings to the Antwerp banker Nicolas Jonghelink. They represent the months of the year and were originally intended for a gallery in Jonghelink's luxurious palace in Antwerp. It is now generally assumed that the months were dealt with two by two and that Bruegel consequently delivered six paintings and not twelve as one might have assumed. Only five of these are still extant, the sixth having either been lost or never completed. Bruegel must have painted most of them in the course of the foregoing year, since Jonghelink had already put them up as collateral in February 1565. In the course of that same year, Bruegel also completed three other paintings and at least four important drawings. This work represents the first broad synthesis of all that had been ripening ever since his return to Antwerp ten years earlier.

The Haymakers (May–June), *The Harvest* (July–August), *The Return of the Herd* (September–October), *The Hunters in the Snow* (November–December), and *The Dark Day* (January–February) are all large paintings, approximately 118 cm high and 160 wide. The scale is a comfortable one for Bruegel, and it allows him to develop the full scope of the landscape while filling it with a host of minute narrative details. This minuteness of detail also forces the viewer to draw close to the painting, so that the broader landscape fills his or her entire field of vision. Thus the viewer feels drawn into it, part of its space and climate. Reproductions inevitably reduce the scale of such large works, thus failing to render this important effect.

This is the first innovation one may notice in comparing these paintings with earlier sequences devoted to the months such as, for instance, those found in *Les Très Riches Heures du Duc de Berry*. The latter work is a sequence of landscapes in miniature, a jewel that can be held in the hollow of the hand. Thus does the world rest in the hand of God, and his lands, in the legitimate hands of the duke. Bruegel's world, by its scale and disposition, unfolds a much broader universe—it even seems to overflow the limits of the frame and to draw us on into the valleys and perspectives that lie hidden beyond its visible horizon.

The medieval miniature can also be seen as the expression of a vertical hierarchy: Above, we have the castle, lifting its crenellated tracery to the heavens; below it lie the land and the work of the fields, and capping it all with its golden signs on a blue ground, the immutable sequence of the zodiac stands like a warranty of the durable order governing this nether world. This stratification is no longer found in Bruegel's work. Things are ordered differently, in an unhierarchical manner, rendered by diagonal lines of force that inflect both the organization of the painted surface and the depths of its perspective. The heavens that spread above are those of a changing climate, good or bad, whose influence is everywhere apparent, starting in the foreground where men are seen at work or play, and reaching all the way into the background where tall crags loom that embody some of the more abrupt and ominous aspects of nature. They appear intractable in certain paintings, while in others they melt away into the golden mildness of the harvest. Such are the two poles of these big works: "Here"

we encounter man in the familiar intimacy of his body as he strains for his livelihood; "there" it is nature that stands before us in its diversity—the remote distance and its charm, the irrevocability of space, and its sometimes serene, sometimes disastrous indifference to man. The exclusive reign of the Subject (in other words of God) meant that space, in a sense (in a very important sense), was of no more than a hierarchical significance—consider the topography of Dante. "God is everywhere" means, among other things, that no soul is ever alone (except the sinner banished from the Presence), nor is any ever truly lost or adrift in the indifferent expanse of the world. The assertion that "God is everywhere" can thus be seen as the negation of the otherwise tragic realities of space and of time, the negation of the unbending seriousness of nature as a real power in human destiny. For if the fall of the sparrow is indeed noted by the heavenly choirs, nature does not share the same concern—hurricanes and earthquakes (as Voltaire observed) show a dreadful indifference to the fate of sparrows and of men. The study of nature, then, is above all the scrupulous study of space and time, and of man in his bodily reality, which depends on both of these.

The supernatural, whose absolute rule now ceased to be the sole and fundamental theme of art, had formerly proposed the awesome order of an eternity without time and of a spiritual world with space. This is what religious art represented either as something that already existed in the immediate present or that was yet to come after the apocalyptic conclusion of all history. This powerful twofold negation was originally an attempt to find an answer to questions that the fact of time and the fact of space inevitably raise within the emotional obscurity of our being—the fact (in terms of human experience and of emotional sensibility) of death seen as a consequence of time, and the fact of solitude seen as a consequence of space. The solution in the former perspective was, as far as possible, to deny that either one has any power over man. But when one's goal becomes the "imitation of nature" (a notion that might remind one, in quite another perspective, of "the Imitation of Christ"), time and space become irreducible realities that confront man and hold him *bodily* in their grip. And this could imply that an even more imperious motive had appeared for developing the celebrated Renaissance perspective and for taking as minute an interest as the Italians did in the anatomy of the human body.

In view of the period he lived in, and all we have so far observed in Bruegel's work, we cannot presume to view the innovations we have come across as merely formal inventions. Bruegel organized his pictorial space in this characteristic way not simply because he wished to achieve a good resemblance of the view he had chosen to paint (indeed, with only one or two exceptions, Bruegel appears to have taken little interest in views as such). He did not despise resemblance, of course, but "nature" aroused his interest not merely as a setting or a spectacle but as the visible nexus of time, space, and man's fundamentally corporeal being—as the very locus and condition, one might say, of man's fate. This also casts a different and highly significant light on Bruegel's concern with peasants, in other words with those men and women who, more than all others, were daily and practically destined to experience this confrontation with nature—with the reign and the power of the Object, one might say.

As a result of this, Bruegel does not paint for *show* but for *meaning*. In doing so, he appeals not to the abstract and theoretical faculties of his spectators but, on the contrary, to their emotional and intuitive perception, to that imaginary region within ourselves where (and this constitutes an additional problem for the artist) neither time nor space can penetrate unless they have first been transposed through some symbolic mediation. The deepest forms of imagination are timeless. Since time itself is beyond imagining on this level, it can only be expressed in terms of pictorial *space*. Space itself, on the other hand, does not find its proper expression through the seemingly obvious mediation of perspective, but it depends, rather, on the kinetic empathy we come to feel for the *human activities* portrayed.[1] In other words, the viewer's perception of space arises out of the activities of some human figure going about his business inside the picture.

Bruegel's narrative technique can strike one as instantly delightful. There is so much to see. In *The Hunters in the Snow*, the figures moving away from us in the foreground and heading on down into the landscape draw our eyes after them and involve us in their world. Their attitudes and gait (and the attitudes and gait of their dogs) convey all we need to know about the way they experience the world. We can almost sense the penetrating cold, the weariness in their bones, the long effort of the day, the nearness of home, and the anticipation of the chores that still remain to be done before nightfall. Bruegel's space is ordered by a trajectory that the eye can follow (just as in his first landscape drawings), the trajectory taken, for instance, by the bird hovering in midflight toward the center of the painting. But it is also perceptible as the space in which a physical effort unfolds, or at very least as the space into which our eyes are induced to follow an exploratory path through the painting—and this approach has little in common with the immobile, blissful contemplation or the thunderstruck reverence induced by the work of some other painters. The figures in the foreground stand before one as the expression of a subjective experience as they go trudging off slowly into the wordless silence of the world and its duration—a world both benign in the midzone of the painting and hostile in the distance. The world into which these people can be seen descending at this historic juncture of the sixteenth century is that of a nature neither human nor divine—though it may seem almost infinite in space. In contrast to this the human presence can be perceived both as an inward solitude and an outward community. And then there is this tremendous expanse in time. As the pictorial space suggests, it extends far beyond the limited frame of our lives and raises, not an immediate threat, but a distant and unconquerable cliff face at the outermost limit of each individual horizon.

Such an analysis can only appear valid when it is applied to an art that strives in some way to articulate an "image of destiny." This has not been the common undertaking of all art, to be sure, though it is certainly the mark of all that is most deeply engaging in art. Aside from the familiar and abundant narrative content encountered here, which serves, in an easily comprehensible form (comparable to the melodic element in a symphony), to punctuate and reinforce the implicit content and overall structure of the painting, Bruegel's way of dealing with landscape presents one with a quite novel figure or ikon of destiny, together with a new formulation of the question of meaning that he first expressed in the powerful if dated idiom of a traditional rhetoric in *The Triumph of Death*.

The imitation of nature in the mid-sixteenth century could no doubt imply a craftsmanlike concern with the accurate rendering of the sights of the world. But for an artist who, like Bruegel, put "more thought than painting" into his work, it also implied that he gave his unreserved attention to an entirely new set of questions—questions that inevitably took on a particular significance once it had been realized that "nature" (as I have presented it here) is neither *mere* scenery nor the *merely* abstract locus in which some sacred drama unfolds, but that it has always been man's sole and proper place and the milieu in which, from the very outset, he is organically rooted. It was this realization that showed nature to be both a decisive force and a fundamental problem confronting human understanding.

[1] See, for instance, the innovative conclusions proposed by the psychoanalyst Sami-Ali in *L'Espace Imaginaire*, Paris, Gallimard, 1978.

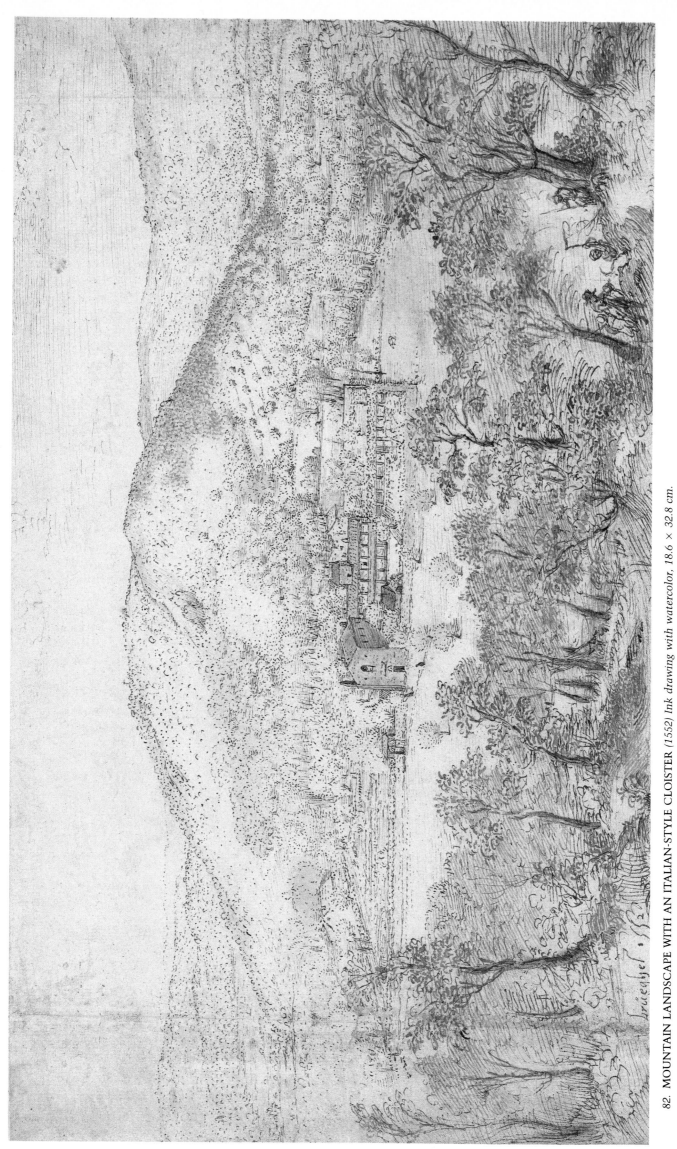

82. MOUNTAIN LANDSCAPE WITH AN ITALIAN-STYLE CLOISTER *(1552) Ink drawing with watercolor, 18.6 × 32.8 cm.*

83. LANDSCAPE WITH WALLED TOWN (1553) Ink drawing, 23.7 × 35.5 cm.

84. ALPINE LANDSCAPE (1553) *Ink drawing, 23.6 × 34.3 cm.*

85. ALPINE LANDSCAPE WITH TWO MULES *(1555–1556) Ink drawing, 29.4 × 43.5 cm.*

86. ALPINE LANDSCAPE WITH AN ARTIST SKETCHING *(1555–1556) Ink drawing, 27.7 × 39.6 cm.*

88. THE HAYMAKERS *Detail: Basket bearers (half the original size).*

89. **THE HAYMAKERS** *(1565). Oil on wood panel, 114 × 158 cm. (See overleaf)*

90. **THE HAYMAKERS** *Detail: the hay wain (half the original size).*

91. SPRING *(1565) Ink drawing, 22.3 × 28.9 cm (reproduced at the scale of the original).*

92. THE HARVEST *(1565) Oil on wood panel, 117 × 163 cm.*

93. SUMMER (1568) *Ink drawing, 22 × 28.5 cm (reproduced at the scale of the original).*

94. THE RETURN OF THE HERD (1568) *Oil on wood panel, 117 × 159 cm.*

95. THE RETURN OF THE HERD *Detail.*

96. THE DARK DAY *Detail.*

97. THE DARK DAY (1565) *Oil on Canvas, 118 × 163 cm.*

98. THE HUNTERS IN THE SNOW *Detail.*

99. THE HUNTERS IN THE SNOW *(1565) Oil on wood panel, 117 × 162 cm.*

100. LANDSCAPE WITH
RABBIT HUNTERS
*(1566) The only copper-
plate engraving done by
Bruegel himself, 22 ×
29 cm.*

101. THE SKATERS BEFORE
SAINT GEORGE'S
GATE *(1559) Copper-
plate engraving by Jan
Galle.*

V. – The Anonymity of the Light

The great diversity of religious subjects presents the artist with a very wide choice as soon as he approaches this domain; one may therefore suppose that Bruegel's choice has some significance and is not due to chance. Who were the people who commissioned works from Bruegel? Van Mander mentions Bruegel's friends Franckert and Abraham Ortels, the banker Nicolas Jonghelink, and finally the city of Brussels—though this last commission was never completed.[1] His immediate clients seem to have been wealthy burghers or scholars who, unlike the aristocracy, did not have any particular reason to stick to a punctilious orthodoxy. The religious struggle that marked this century was further complicated, as we have seen, by economic, political, and social conflicts. The special interests of each social class can be sensed at work behind the veil of vigorous religious polemics. The party in power was Catholic like the king himself. The nobles and the bourgeoisie were drawn to Luther's arguments, which questioned the authority of the foreign power that they themselves opposed. Craftsmen, peasants, and workers, finally, were more inclined to the Calvinist austerity that seemed more radical than Luther's and hostile to the religious images whose power and prestige upheld the authority of the king and of Rome.

Bruegel, while hardly inclined to get involved in polemics himself, was an attentive observer of life, and he must have sensed the interests that fueled the various doctrinal arguments. His closeness to Ortels and his circle, together with all that we know of his work, suggests that he had no sympathy for the doctrinal intransigence found on either side. All the time he lived in Antwerp, he had been surrounded with a spirit of tolerance. Today such tolerance strikes us as the mark of a reasonable person, but this was hardly the case in an age in which every doctrine had become a banner that one either had to fight or serve. It was for this tolerant circle, we may suppose, that Bruegel produced his last sequence of religious work.

This series distinguishes itself from the earlier one in that it deals with a quite different problem. The first series responded to the sardonic query of triumphant death and sought to give expression, through a religious idiom, to a representation of life that would be illuminated with some ultimate meaning. The second series shows the artist faced with a new challenge: Meaning

Old peasant woman (1564)

may well shine forth, but anguish, folly, intolerance, and narrow, short-term interests will always strive to monopolize it and to manipulate people by using it to their immediate advantage. They will turn meaning into an instrument of domination and persecution, pervert it, and even press its luminous seduction into the service of the unmeaning death. Now it happens that the very religion that Bruegel's century had turned into an instrument of war is based on a gospel that contains some exemplary condemnations of all intolerance, of all base forms of intransigence. When Bruegel deals with these subjects, he does not take sides in the polemics of the day—he was not involved in a "struggle" against such or such a power, whether lay or religious. But he did add a discreet and indispensable note to the intellectual climate of the day, and he spoke a language his friends could understand, without running the risk of unduly provoking the Thought Police or the intractable partisans of either side. The first series, as we have seen, begins with the grisaille *The Resurrection*, which might be regarded as the epigraph to what was yet to come. The second series also begins with a grisaille that once again appears to anticipate the answer that Bruegel wished to formulate. This time the subject is *Christ and the Adulterous Woman* (1565) a work that most critics today acknowledge to be an authentic Bruegel.

The work is exceptional from a formal point of view, for here Bruegel presents nothing but standing figures without the usual broad landscape in the background. Something of an Italian influence can be sensed here, and more particularly the influence of Raphael. To understand what Bruegel is driving at one must know something of the evangelical narrative (John, chapter 8) that it illustrates. This is a work that always remained in the artist's possession (his son Jan later received it in inheritance), a work that Bruegel chose to paint at a time of heightened religious intransigence, and it is easy enough to grasp the underlying message once the subject of the painting is known. Once again it is not a polemical work, but a focus for reflection that Bruegel kept at home, as

---

[1] And possibly Cardinal Granvelle. He may have acquired his Bruegel paintings indirectly. The months that Bruegel painted for Jonghelink became the property of the city of Antwerp, which, in turn, offered them to the emperor. It is also apparent that Bruegel painted a number of works without waiting for a commission: *Christ and the Adulterous Woman*, for instance, or *The Magpie on the Gallows*, which he left to his wife.

though to invest the house with its message of moderation.[2]

That same year (1565) he also painted *The Unfaithful Shepherd* whose subject is drawn from the Gospel according to St. John.[3] This much is clear: The painting we now know is either an original or was derived from an original painted by Bruegel himself; this is apparent in the monumental treatment of the main figure, so characteristic of his later period, and also in that of the landscape, which has much in common with the landscape of *The Misanthropist*. So the painting must be examined here, regardless of whether it actually is by Bruegel's hand (as some experts claim) or only a copy (as others maintain). Despite its evangelical theme, it tends to be outside the realm of religious painting and may be regarded as an anticipation of the somber works of 1568. It should nonetheless be examined in the present chapter to the extent that it represents the meditations of a tolerant man, deeply concerned by the religious persecutions and disorders then afflicting the Netherlands. This painting apparently had a pendant depicting *The Good Shepherd* who gives his life for his sheep. Unfortunately, the surviving copy is only an awkward imitation that hardly allows us to guess at what the original work may have looked like.

Aside from the desolation of the landscape, the surprising thing about *The Unfaithful Shepherd* is the forcefulness with which movement is rendered. The deep ruts that run straight to the horizon seem to suggest that the landscape itself is slipping away, whereas the imposing, Michelangelesque mass of the shepherd seems to confer some stability at least to this rout of space in a desolate moor. This painting consequently should be regarded as a turning point through which Bruegel emerges from a period of religious interrogation, enters into a phase of purely secular bitterness, and reaches beyond that to an entirely stoic solution that calls upon the resilience and resourcefulness of men without making any clear reference to the beyond.

Preaching of John the Baptist (detail, 1565)

The Preaching of John the Baptist (1565) is usually regarded as a representation, under the outward form of an evangelical subject, of a scene then familiar in the Netherlands: the clandestine religious meetings that might easily assemble four or five thousand people at a time—common folk, no doubt, but also merchants and nobles. The painting depicts a varied crowd. The diversity of costumes reveals the wide range of social classes, and one can recognize monks, burghers, peasants, and other men and women of the people, together with a Gypsy, wearing a striped blanket and reading the palm of one of the listeners in the foreground. A good number of people have climbed up into the trees to get a better view—a familiar sight at such gatherings, one chronicler reports. One need not consider this painting as a statement in favor of the Calvinist doctrine that was propagated at such meetings. Bruegel, some years earlier, attended country weddings in order to observe the manners and attitudes of the peasants, and we can easily imagine him taking off into the woods with his family, impelled by a desire to see, hear, and understand things that were stirring up such interest at the time.

The ostensible subject is a quite different one, of course. John the Baptist appears in the gospels as the precursor of Christ—the man who prepares the way for him and heralds his coming. He withdrew into a wilderness near the Jordan River (represented in the background), and he baptized people there, dipping his converts into the river as he would in a ritual bath. His mission was to ready people for the coming of the Messiah, the savior who was widely awaited and who would finally resolve all the contradictions inherent in human destiny. The crowds can be seen pressing around John, and in the midst of them, stands Jesus. Nothing in particular seems to distinguish him from all the others, but John points him out: "Behold the one who is to come."[4]

The panel is as wide as the biggest of Bruegel's paintings (160 cm), but (at 95 cm) it is no longer as high as it originally was. As can be seen from copies by Jan Bruegel and Peter the Younger, some 20 cm have been cut off the top, and a bit less, off the bottom. This tends to upset the delicate balance of the composition, which takes the form of a double pyramid: The first stands on its head

---

[2] According to Mosaic law, adultery was punishable by death. The guilty parties were led out of town, and those who felt so inclined were free to stone them to death. Jesus, then, was in the Temple in Jerusalem, teaching in the midst of the large crowds that were coming and going about the broad courtyard. His presence there displeased the orthodox legislators and theologians whom Jesus had often criticized before. They, therefore, imagined (the gospel says) a provocation that would force him to take a stand on an uncomfortable issue. With some luck it might be possible to bar his access to the Temple and even to have him detained. So they brought before him a married woman who had been surprised with her lover. Jesus was asked for his opinion: "In the law Moses has laid down that such women are to be stoned. What do you say about it?" Jesus ignored them, and leaning down, he began to draw lines in the dust. The other repeated their question, and Jesus lifted his head. The law says she must be stoned? he asked. Very well, then: "That one of you who is faultless shall throw the first stone." Then he bent down again and resumed writing on the ground. When they heard what he had said (the story relates), one by one they went away, "the eldest first." After a while, in the bustle of the great courtyard, Jesus found himself alone with the woman. "Where are they? Has no one condemned you?" "No one, sir," she said. "No more do I," Jesus replied.

[3] "I am the good shepherd. The good shepherd lays down his life for the sheep. The hireling, when he sees the wolf coming, abandons his sheep and runs away.... Then the wolf harries the flock and scatters the sheep." (John 10:11–12)

[4] A minute detail in the background depicts the baptism of Christ and the descending dove.

120

The Census in Bethlehem
(detail, 1566)

and has as its apex the figure wearing a "Chinese" hat at the center of the foreground; the second culminates in the figure of Christ. John himself is off center in relation to the composition as a whole, but the fact that everybody in the painting is looking toward him still makes him the somewhat unstable center of the work. This oscillation between Jesus and John reveals the remarkably subtle way in which Bruegel's composition expresses the latent significance of his work.

The composition of this painting, along with that of *The Way to Calvary* and of other works discussed in the present chapter, is something unique in the history of art. The medieval treatment of a religious subject tended to place the main figure at the center and to make him somewhat larger than the others. Italian art, and all the religious works that followed the guidelines set down by the Counter-Reformation, favored a forthright presentation of the main subject in the foreground in a setting that was relatively free of accessory matters (compared to the swarming density of Bruegel's works), or even in some quasi-abstract space in which only the holy figure or the significant gesture were presented in a clearly dramatized form. The presentation that is so characteristic of Bruegel (and of some of his precursors and contemporaries) is typical of an age of transition in which all former certainties could appear shaken. I suspect this is why we appreciate him so much today. For something has become apparent to us that tended to escape ages armed with unshakable convictions: A truth that asserts itself as unequivocal and triumphant can already be considered a lie. Such a notion is entirely compatible with Bruegel's view, according to which, the most significant event is one that unfolds in hiding.

This brings a somewhat different and more elaborate articulation to the question that is the point of departure of this series of paintings. The anonymity or "incognito" of the light (as Ernst Bloch calls it) is a recurrent theme in various cultures, notably in Jewish thought at various periods, and it is also inherent to nascent Christianity, since this faith presents the Son of God being born on a stable floor, predictably enough rejected by the notables and leaders of the community, and dying among malefactors. This is the notion to which Bruegel seems to be giving expression in his treatment of his great religious works in which the incarnate Meaning, which is come to save the human spirit from the grip of a triumphant absurdity, is shown passing furtively through the crowd without being recognized. One is reminded of the Old Testament text that the authors of the gospels were pleased to quote: "The stone which the builders refused is become the head stone of the corner" (Psalms 118:22). The interesting thing about Bruegel is that he appears to consider this adventure of the light, appearing unrecognized (incognito) in the darkness of the world, as a fundamental pattern in no way restricted to the religious realm, a constant of experience in general, to which the religious matter merely provides a symbolic key. Unlike most other artists dealing with religious subjects, who try to elevate the obscurity of daily experience toward the simplifying light of dogma, Bruegel seems to want to bring this light down into the teeming complexity and anonymous obscurity of a material world that the powers of arms, finance, and the law are always striving to subdue. So Bruegel is in fact putting forward a philosophical thesis and expressing it with imposing simplicity. The light that breaks out and brings its share of meaning to the future is not only the Jesus of the Christians (to whom Bruegel undoubtedly addressed his prayers) but also every human spirit and initiative by which all such power and authority is troubled—the creative disorder that the builders would be happy to cast aside and destroy, but that remains the sole true hope of the world of man.

This is what Bruegel affirms. But he does so in such a universal, transparent, and human tone that none can take exception. The only risk he incurs is that of an encounter with indifferent minds who will view him with the same condescension they grant each creative impetus that emerges and anonymously passes among us, unheralded by the thunder of rhetoric, unescorted by the storm clouds of Sinai.

The Census in Bethlehem (1566) illustrates a passage from the Gospel according to St. Luke.[5] The scene is a Brabantine village under the snow. The tax collector has decided to take advantage of the occasion to collect his tithe, and a crowd is swarming in front of his window to the left. A panel hanging against the wall next to the window bears the two-headed eagle of the Hapsburgs. Toward the center and in the background people are pressing around a fire to warm themselves. A large hollow tree serves as the village pub—its name, as we see, is the Golden Swan. The local inn is full, and that, as the evangelist explains, is why Mary had to give birth in a stable as soon as she reached town. A red sun sets behind the sharp black branches of the largest tree while children continue throwing snowballs in the twilight and skating on the pond. At the bottom center of the painting, with nothing in particular to distinguish them, we can recognize Joseph by the saw slung over his shoulder (he is a

---

[5] "In those days a decree was issued by the Emperor Augustus for a general registration throughout the Roman world. This was the first registration of its kind; it took place when Quirinus was governor of Syria. For this purpose everyone made his way to his own town; and so Joseph went up to Judea from the town Nazareth in Galilee, to be registered in the city of David called Bethlehem . . . and with him went Mary who was betrothed to him." (Luke 2:1–5)

carpenter), followed by the ox and the ass mentioned by the prophets. Mary, Joseph's pregnant bride, wrapped in a gray blanket and clutching a basket to her, is riding the ass.

The Massacre of the Innocents (1566) was probably conceived as a pendant to *The Census in Bethlehem.* Some art historians believe that the painting is not wholly by Bruegel's hand, but all agree that it is a faithful rendering of his conception. The setting is once more a snowbound Brabantine village. The main street is filled with soldiers. Some break down doors, while other slit the throats of little children. To the right, a mounted herald, his tabard embroidered with the Hapsburg eagle, is hemmed in by pleading men and women, but he can only spread his hands in a helpless gesture. As Georges Marlier observed, Bruegel must have witnessed, perhaps not a massacre, but at least a similar raid by Spanish troops, for the scene is handled with much restraint, and the attitudes seem entirely right and are devoid of any theatrical pathos. Both works touch upon the same themes of the anonymity of the light and the violent repression of its emerging power.

Adoration of the Magi in Winter (1567) is in the same mood as the two foregoing works and shows the light acknowledged by a few discerning men. The scene is once again a quiet village in wintertime, except that in this one thick snowflakes are falling. As in the *Census,* Bruegel devotes the greater part of the painting to the everyday occupations of the villagers. A fire has been lit in a corner. The weather is freezing. Water has to be fetched up through a hole in the ice; wood is being brought in to heat the house. The falling snow enfolds everything in its cozy intimacy. The shrill shouts and outcries of the world are momentarily muted, and even its angular shapes appear somewhat gentler. It is as though time itself were in suspense in the peculiar, womblike space created by falling flakes.

The Conversion of Saint Paul (1567) is the last painting of the series and Bruegel's last religious work altogether. The theme chosen by Bruegel presents the model of a solution to the problem that had preoccupied the artist ever since he began this series. The Paul we see here is still a stern inquisitor named Saul who is fully determined to stamp out the new Christian sect. The story is related in the Acts of the Apostles (chapter 9). He has, for some time, been tracking down the Christians in Jerusalem, but he has now decided that he should go up to Damascus to pick up the heretics who may have been arrested there and take them back to Jerusalem to be judged. Now 1567, the year in which this work was painted, also happens to have been the year in which political events reached a showdown in the Netherlands. During the preceding year a group of young noblemen of various confessions had presented the regent with a peti-

tion in favor of religious tolerance. They had heard themselves described as "beggars" for their pains; rebellion was ready to break out, though Egmont, de Hornes, and William of Orange still sought to contain it. The first surge of the iconoclastic rampage that destroyed four hundred churches began on the tenth of August 1566. One year later, on the twenty-second of August 1567, the Duke of Alva arrived in the Netherlands with mercenaries fresh from fighting the Moslems. The outbreak of iconoclasm had been the pretext for their coming, but we know something today of which Bruegel and his contemporaries were unaware: The duke's secret instructions, written in Philip II's hand, ordered him to subdue the rebellion without recoiling, if necessary, "before the total destruction of the country." Bruegel did not need any such information to inspire him. Anxiety had been widespread for some time. Starting in August of that year, Bruegel himself may have been required to provide quarters for some of the duke's soldiers.

While Saul was on the road and nearing Damascus, suddenly a light flashed from the sky all around him. He fell to the ground and heard a voice saying: "Saul, Saul, why do you persecute me?" "Tell me, Lord," he said, "who you are." The voice answered: "I am Jesus whom you are persecuting." The setting is once more a grandiose and finely observed Alpine landscape, one of those natural revelations that had dazzled the young traveler on his return from Italy. A deep gorge on one side affords a swooping vista into the plain below. A few puffs of cloud float by in the remote depths. Saul, or Paul, has been thrown to the ground together with his horse, and he can be seen lying there, surrounded by some of his men. One man glances upward, shading his eyes against some invisible glare. Saul has raised his head toward the light that cast him down. The incident has not been noticed by all, and the long line of soldiers ahead keeps moving on. Saul alone has gone through this violent spiritual experience, and he alone will be changed.

Paul must be regarded here as the *type* or cipher Bruegel selected to designate a possible resolution of the problem arising out of human intransigence and its attending brutality. This solution hinges upon the moment in which the incognito is lifted and the light is revealed as light in the fullness of its power. The persecutor is confronted with the tangible reality, the overwhelming charm of what he sought to destroy, and in an instant his whole world topples. But Bruegel, who is deeply pragmatic, also knows that this cannot be a real working solution in this "nether" world—that there is, in fact, *no* ready solution. The virulence of human intolerance remains what it always was, in spite of the splendid model of conversion that Bruegel has built. So in the end he finds himself faced with the more despairing aspects of human nature. This is what he will turn to next.

102. THE PREACHING OF JOHN THE BAPTIST *Detail: St. John center, Christ to the right.*

122

103. THE PREACHING OF JOHN THE BAPTIST *(1565) Oil on wood panel, 95 × 160 cm.*

104. THE PREACHING OF JOHN THE BAPTIST *Detail:
the crowd, in the distance, the baptism of Christ.*

105. CHRIST AND THE ADULTEROUS WOMAN *(1565) Grisaille on wood panel, 24.1 × 34 cm.*

106. **THE MASSACRE OF THE INNOCENTS** *(Some doubt about the attribution to Peter Bruegel.) (1566) Oil on wood panel, 111 × 160 cm.*

107. **THE CENSUS IN BETHLEHEM** *(1566) Oil on wood panel, 116 × 164 cm.*

108. ADORATION OF THE MAGI IN WINTER. *(Some doubt about the attribution to Peter Bruegel.) (1567) Oil on wood panel, 35 × 55 cm.*

109. *Jacques Savery,* SUNRISE OVER A VALLEY *Ink drawing, 14.3 × 18.5 cm. Both date (1561) and signature are spurious. Hans Mielke of the Berlin Kupferstichkabinett has reattributed this work to Jacques Savery. Perhaps inspired by the detail reproduced in il. 114.*

110. THE CONVERSION OF SAINT PAUL *Detail at about 80 percent of the size of the original.*

111. **THE CONVERSION OF SAINT PAUL** *(1567) Oil on wood panel, 108 × 156 cm.*

112. THE UNFAITHFUL SHEPHERD *(copy by Peter Brueghel the Younger) (1565) Oil on wood panel 77 × 88 cm.*

113. THE GOOD SHEPHERD *(copy by Peter Brueghel the Younger) (1565) Oil on wood panel, 40 × 54.5 cm.*

VI. – A Time of Bitterness

The painter and the connoisseur (detail, 1565)

The unkempt artist stands glaring at the world through shaggy brows. His glance is dark, direct, unyielding; his mouth turns down in an expression of anger and disgust. He obviously does not approve of what he sees. He would like to spit out the things his gaze had once so ravenously devoured. Yet he does not turn away. He raises a thick brush in his right hand and the act of painting will allow him to cast off, into the depths of the picture, all the revolting filth he sees crawling about right under his nose.

Behind him stands the connoisseur. He is unaware of the sights that the painter observes. His silly yet seemingly judicious gaze is fixed attentively upon the emerging painting, and his turtle mouth exhales a sigh of restrained delight—how absolutely lovely! Without awaiting any conscious decision, his hand has already reached for the purse. He is determined to buy the painting he has not understood, without even waiting for the paint to dry.

Should this be regarded as a self-portrait? If so, it is obviously a parodic one. But need we really know whether Bruegel's nose had this particular shape and no other, or whether his hair, at forty, was indeed hoary and unwashed? What really does matter is the fact that "The Painter and the Connoisseur" (about 1565 or thereafter) manages to convey, in a detached and humorous tone, the unbridgeable difference between two ways of seeing the world—that of the thoughtful and perceptive man and that of the mere spectator whose insensitive glance, to the artist's obvious irritation, savors the hateful spectacle of human misfortune from a merely esthetic point of view.

The artist, by means of his pictures, can be seen to lend a voice to the silent, suffering flesh of the world. But because this voice says what it has to say with such effortless simplicity, the spectator may easily ignore all that touches upon the fate of this flesh and only attend to the delicate incarnation that glows in Bruegel's work, in the very tone of his utterances.

What are we to make of the man who stands before us here? What remains here of the youth who was once overwhelmed by the deep delight of the world and the many-faceted vitality of mankind? Something seems to have touched and seared him about this time—and it looks as though this painful experience was to remain a burden on his mind for several years to come. The paintings produced during this period are harsher in their intent than ever before, and most of them are compressed into a smaller format than usual. Until now, Bruegel had always viewed the world from above, as would an observer looking out from a high vantage point. Now he stands on the same level as other men, and one senses that something within the man has stiffened as though in pain or in disgust.

Bruegel's "periods" can be seen to arise like waves that overlap. Each fresh wave begins to take shape while the former is still at its height. The new outlook, so full of bitterness, began to appear in 1565; at the time that Bruegel was still working at his last series of religious works. It reached its peak in 1568 with a constellation of paintings that Bruegel produced even as he was already working on the great conceptions of the final phase.

Let us go back for another look at a painting that has already been discussed, *The Unfaithful Shepherd* (1565). It is hardly a religious work. The parable as Bruegel formulates it appears to be no more than an ironic presentation of the *Raison d'État*. The wolf has come? The country is being bled? Well, let it bleed! The plain is empty, and all around a flat, uniform world spreads out like an endless bad dream. The low-lying farmhouse on the horizon cannot even be considered a refuge. There is no place to hide. The landscape has not really shrunk yet, but it has lost all its vitality and relief.

Two equally somber works appear the following year (1566). Both have been lost, and the copies can only yield some rather slight clues to the artist's mood and outlook. *The Robbers* (1566?) is known only through an awkward copy by Peter the Younger. It depicts the very same godforsaken heath, the same ruts, the same farmhouse hunched down in the distance. One might even say it is the same story without the figure of the shepherd. A peasant and his wife play the part of the sheep, and the wolf, in the person of three soldiers armed with lances and pistols, is stripping them of their belongings. The terrified woman must have fallen to her knees as soon as she saw them approaching. One of the soldiers now kicks her in the back. The fellow to the right is carrying off their bundle. That's all there is to it.

The mood conveyed by the copy is unsatisfactory. Copies painted by Peter Brueghel the Younger tend to be marked by rigid attitudes that can at times make the interaction between the characters seem incoherent. One may even get the impression that the painter is trying to turn his peasants into figures of fun, although this would have been quite incompatible with the father's outlook. We must, therefore, draw from the credit accrued to Bruegel the Elder in the rest of his work and suppose that the original was both more forceful in its expression and more desolate in its mood.

The *Peasant Brawl* (also 1566) was copied by both Peter the Younger and Peter Paul Rubens. The latter's drawing restricts itself to the three main figures and stresses the antagonistic turbulence of the movement caught by Bruegel. The copy by the son, on the other hand, is laborious, and as in *The Robbers*, it reduces the movement to an awkward pose. The scene depicts a brawl arising out of a card game on the village square. The bench has been overturned, and one of the men has brought his flail down resoundingly on the other one's back. The latter, meanwhile, has grasped a pitchfork that his wife is trying to wrest from him. A third person attempts to part them, shoving one man away with his shoulder, the other with his foot. Taken out of context the painting could be regarded as merely anecdotal. Rubens must have admired the lively, intelligible, and natural manner in which the movement was set down—and this is what his copy has recorded. It is the only scene of its kind in Bruegel's work, and it appears to have been done in the context of the other small paintings that, under a somewhat more enigmatic form, arise as though in muted counterpoint to the series the artist devoted, at the outset of his career, to various human vices and follies. I have said that Bruegel does not present the sights of the world as something merely spectacular or picturesque, but that he views all things in terms of a meaning or (and this amounts to the same thing) of an absurdity that seeks after some meaning that may redeem it.

Still Bruegel does not look upon all the follies of mankind with equal severity, and one may wonder whether he did not paint *The Land of Plenty* (in 1567) as a tale for his son Peter when the child was three years old. This theme appears in art and literature of that century like a dreamworld of regression in which the dominant and demanding figure of God does not appear. It is mentioned, for instance, in a text plagiarized from Rabelais and published in 1538: "How Panurge came upon a flat country that, though never ploughed, is very fertile, where hot meat pies do grow; & of a cloud from out of which roast skylarks fall, & of how the roofs are made out of hot pies." (Chapter XIX) R.-H. Marijnissen and M. Seidel, who quote this text, have also found a description of this country in a Dutch text published in 1546. According to this text, this "Luyeleckerlandt" (the Cloud-Cuckoo-Land of Aristophanes) can only be reached by eating one's way through a mountain of buckwheat gruel. The roofs there are covered with pancakes and tarts; the hedges are braided sausage and black pudding; the rivers are all of milk, and capons walk about roasted to a turn. Each of these traits are found in Bruegel's painting, but the author of the book does not leave well enough alone and concludes with a sententious reproof of laziness and gluttony: "The place is of ill-repute, best known to scoundrels and to all those who have no care for decency and virtue."

Still, a person may dream, and surely a tiny regression can do no harm on occasion. It is also significant that the drink found in this country is none of your adult's wine or beer, but only the milk that children love. And every child well knows that his soft-boiled egg makes its way onto the table by its own mysterious means, and that food finds its way into his mouth on its own, even when mother happens to be holding the spoon. A print derived from this work shows the helmeted man on the left holding his mouth wide open to receive an incoming (roast) skylark that can no longer be made out on the painting.

No matter whether or not the work was actually painted for a child, what counts is that it speaks distinctly to the child who, in every adult, remains the ideal reader of all children's books. There is both humor and good-natured irony, but no pedantic morality in this work. Indeed, the very thought of a moral would seem ludicrous. And one might also wonder whether such a work does not echo a constant and legitimate fear of hunger—even though the peasantry of the Netherlands, unlike that of France, was quite prosperous in those days. What is striking about this work is that it is the first expression of a reverie concerning human well-being here below—a reverie that might indeed strike one as a parody of all the consolations of Heaven. At this point it is still no more than a reverie and a reminiscence of a time in childhood when food and clothing seemed to appear spontaneously, wherever the need was felt. Later on one would come to expect not so much food without effort but that effort should at least provide each man with his food. For the sixteenth century, with Thomas More and Tommaso Campanella, is also the century of the first utopias, of which all the Lands of Plenty may be considered the hollow, anticipatory dream form.

The Bird's-nester, The Misanthropist, The Beggars—and we should also add the drawing of *The Beekeepers*—are works to which we have lost the key. Here the spectator is once more on ground level and enclosed in a relatively limited space. The bird's-nester is up in a tree robbing a nest. He is losing his hat but not otherwise in danger. The bag lying on the ground is probably intended to carry off his take. But what is to be made of the monumental figure of a rustic "Kasper Hauser" standing at the center of the painting, holding a pike in his right hand and extending his left index towards the nest robber? He seems to be paying no attention to where he is going and may well fall into the water at any moment. To the left, behind the birches, stands a farm. Another one, with a duck pond, can be seen off to the right.

An explanation of sorts may be afforded by an examination of the drawing of *The Beekeepers*. Here too we can make out a bird's-nester climbing up a tree while the hooded figures with wicker masks busy themselves with the hives from which, one may suppose, they are removing the honey. An inscription, bottom left, quotes a Flemish proverb: *Dye den nest weet dyen weeten / dyen rooft dy heeten*—"To know of the nest is but to know /to carry it off is to have it." Some authors sense a political allusion. The idea is quite plausible, and viewed in this light, the drawing appears intelligible enough—but what about the painting? The work does not seem to provide any further clues, and its enigmatic character might in itself be considered a good argument in favor of a topical interpretation. A wealthy financier, reduced to political impotence by the military presence of Spain and hampered by higher taxes might well have sought a form of symbolic release to his irritation by displaying such a painting in the privacy of his home. In the same vein, I well remember an old and fiercely patriotic English nanny who, walking through the streets during a visit to Hitler's Germany, daily acknowledged the countless mandatory Nazi salutes by raising her right arm in the approved fashion and defiantly muttering "to Hell with Hitler!"

The Misanthropist brings us back to the landscape of *The Unfaithful Shepherd* and *The Robbers*—only here the sheep are peacefully grazing while the shepherd leans on his crooks. The manner of presentation may remind one of *The Proverbs*, with two figures acting out an expression: *Om da de werelt is soe ongetru / Daer om gha ic in den ru* ("For that the world is so untrue / Therefore do I go about in rue") says the inscription. The main figure is that of an old man wearing a cape rather like that of the *pleureurs* (or mourners) that surround certain Gothic tombs (that of Philip Pot, for instance, end of fifteenth century, in the Louvre). Behind him another man is squatting inside a sphere topped by a cross such as we have already seen used in *The Proverbs* to signify "the World." So it is "the World" in the shape of a ragged beggar that is lifting the old man's purse. E. Michel suggests that this figure may have been added at a later date (which would also imply that the folds of the black cloak were repainted at the point where they are lifted by the purse strings). Finally, a good number of nails with multiple points, such as the military use even today to puncture tires, have been strewn on the ground before the old man. Here too, unless we take the painting at face value as the literal rendering of a stock phrase, Bruegel's intention is not entirely clear.

The Cripples is one of Bruegel's smallest paintings (18 × 21 cm) and it too raises a number of difficulties. We may note the closed perspective, the unusually low viewpoint, the figure, moving off to the right, similar to those taking up the collection in the Orson and Valentine or Mopsus and Nisa groups of *The Battle of Carnival and Lent*. The same cripples are to be seen there too, wearing fox tails, a distinctive sign, we are told, for lepers. Despite the agitated movement of their stunted limbs and of their crutches and prostheses, which might suggest a dance, the cripples look as though they were about to part. They are wearing a variety of head dresses that have suggested a number of interpretations. The man to the right, for instance, has a bishop's mitre, the one to the left, a sort of crenellated tarboosh that might conceivably represent a crown. The headgear of the other three should, in this view, make them personifications of the soldier, the burgher, and the peasant. But even if this were true, it still would not be of much help to those who wish to understand the deeper significance of the painting.

Bruegel is obviously portraying the wretched fate of countless men and women of his time. The grotesqueness of these contorted bodies and faces is weirdly potent, and Bruegel's strength lies in his straightforward objectivity, tempered neither by derision nor by commiseration. One may suppose that he is attracted to these mutilated forms by the driving force of life and its terrible persistence, which they personify. Bruegel's own period may not have seen things in this light, and each spectator could, if he wished, find cause for laughter in these twisted silhouettes. But Bruegel himself does not take such matters into account. *"Et faisoit-on grant risée, pour ce que c'estoient tous gens de povre estat,"* wrote a fifteenth-century chronicler: "And there was much mockery, for they were all people of low estate." He was describing the death by torture of a band of brigands. Huizinga, who quotes this sentence, goes on to give another example of the cruelty (often mingled with naïve commiseration) that marked the daily life of the period: "In 1425, an 'esbatement' takes place in Paris, of four blind beggars, armed with sticks, with which they hit each other in vying for a pig that is a prize of the combat. On the evening before, they are led through the town, all armed, with a great banner in front, on which was pictured a pig, and preceded by a man playing the bagpipes."

Bruegel's treatment of physical infirmities is marked by a sharp and uncomplacent realism. His humanism is fundamentally stoic and down to earth. This is apparent in *The Parable of the Blind*, a painting whose import is quite clear since we are familiar with the source of its narrative material. It illustrates a parable from the Gospel according to St. Luke (6:39), significantly joined to another text concerning the eye: "He also offered them a parable: 'Can one blind man be guide to another? Will they not both fall into the ditch? . . . Why do you look at the speck of sawdust in your brother's eye, with never a thought to the great plank in your own? . . . You hypocrite! First take the plank out of your own eye, and then you will see clearly to take the speck out of your brother's.' "

It does seem rather surprising that these clinically observed faces of blind men should have been the first true portraits Bruegel actually produced. The faces in *The Adoration of the Magi* do, of course, have the quality of portraits, but they are treated more in the manner of a dramatic characterization. Bruegel must have studied these blind men most attentively, taking note of their bodily attitudes, the condition of the eye, the slack tone of the facial muscles that is found in people who do not commu-

Carnival and Lent (detail, 1563)

nicate through the expressive movement of their features. Bruegel's painting is a naturalistic rendering of Christ's parable, which, once again, as in *The Unfaithful Shepherd*, can be applied to a variety of subjects: churches, governments, and, above all, the familiar and Erasmian "folly" of mankind. The circumstances are pathetic and absurd, the scene painfully realistic and undeniably didactic in intent.[1] Indeed, this bleak and uncompromising painting may well provide the most concise presentation of Bruegel's views at this stage of his life. He seems to be standing quite outside any religious reference, in spite of the evangelical text that has served as his point of departure. Commentators have dwelt at length on Bruegel's "pessimism," though it might seem more appropriate to place this mood in a somewhat broader and more complex perspective than that of mere pessimism or optimism.

Another work, *The Fall of Icarus*, may appear rather close to this one in terms of content, though its mood is ostensibly quite different. It seems appropriate to discuss it here, even though historians fail to agree on its date and even on its degree of authenticity. The craft is obviously inferior, says one, and so it has to be a work of Bruegel's youth. You are right about the craft, another replies, but the overall conception is quite splendid, and so it must be a copy (by a pupil?) of an original work that has since been lost. The limpid organization of the pictorial discourse does indeed suggest a mature work. And a certain affinity of outlook with the paintings done in 1568 seems to justify my decision to place the work in their company and examine it in this chapter.

The story is borrowed from Greek mythology and, more specifically, from Ovid's *Metamorphoses*, though Bruegel, as usual, brings in some original variants of his own.[2] The view of nature that this work implies is already quite modern and, to the extent that Bruegel sees

nature as a splendid and indifferent presence, definitely in contrast with the former (medieval) conception. In the endless expanse of the world that Bruegel unfolds in this painting, the figure of Icarus is reduced to a hand and two legs that can still be made out projecting above the waves, while five or six feathers hover down at a more leisurely pace. Nor is nature the only indifferent entity here: A shepherd, a sailor, a fisherman, and a ploughman, utterly absorbed in their tasks, have noticed neither the flight nor the fall (an entirely enigmatic figure has also been discovered, lying flat on his back a bit higher than the horse's head). Ovid's unmerciful partridge is perched on a branch (just beneath the legs); it cocks its eye at the viewer, taking him to witness, in the manner of the moralist in the earlier didactic prints. The landscape, a splendid, tender vision of radiant remoteness, is flooded with a gentle light that stands in pathetic contrast to the general indifference surrounding the fall. The sun, instead of being at its zenith, as one might expect, is already setting on the horizon, as though Icarus had begun his fall from such a dizzying height that it has taken him half the day to reach the sea. The theme of ambitious venture, *hubris*, and fall applies to all human endeavor, and perhaps, in Bruegel's view here, more particularly to the life venture of the artist. Had not Bruegel himself soared high above the world, seeking the broadest conceivable view? And here, in the penultimate phase of his art, we seem to find him, cast down and brooding bitterly among the stones and thorns, but also among the blind passions of a society in crisis that naturally fails to sense the artist's scope as it goes stumbling into the ditch.

All these works might be regarded as the profane response to the sequence of religious paintings that preceded them. As we have seen, one cannot always be sure of the significance of each one of these works nor even, in certain cases, of their date, but to the extent that the uncertainty allows us to reach some conclusion, this would seem the appropriate way of approaching them. Voicing his feelings in a tone that is by turns bitter and lyrical, Bruegel submits his painful survey of the negative aspects of life: human "folly," indifference, moral blindness, and finally the unbreachable indifference of nature itself.

---

[1] The church in this painting has been identified as that of Pede-Saint-Anne in the Province of Brabant. Similarities between this landscape and the others dealt with in this chapter would seem to suggest that Bruegel spent some time in the country during the year 1568. His absence from the studio may also account for the small scale of most of these paintings. *The Parable of the Blind* is much larger, of course, but it is done on canvas (as is *The Misanthrope*), possibly because this made it easier to carry back to Brussels.

[2] Having built the labyrinth commissioned by King Minos of Crete as a prison for the Minotaur (a monster half human and half bull), the architect Daedalus was confined to the island with his son Icarus. They managed to escape thanks to the wings Daedalus made out of feathers, wax, and thread. Icarus, however, ecstatic with joy, flew ever higher despite his father's warnings. As he approached the sun, the wax that held his wings together melted, and Icarus plummeted into the sea. Ovid mentions a ploughman, a shepherd, and a fisherman who marveled to see men flying and took them for gods. He also mentions a

---

partridge that beat its wings and rejoiced in the boy's fall. For, Ovid explains, Daedalus' first teacher in his youth had been a sage named Perdrix, inventor of the saw and of the compass, and Daedalus, jealous of his accomplishments, had pushed him off a tower. But the goddess Minerva intervened and changed Perdrix into a partridge, covering his body with feathers as he fell. The fall of Icarus is thus presented as Perdrix's revenge. But Bruegel, as we have seen, makes a much subtler use of the ironic bird.

114. THE FALL OF ICARUS *Detail: the fall.*

115. **THE FALL OF ICARUS** *(1555–1568?) Oil on canvas, 73.5 × 112 cm.*

116. PEASANT BRAWL *(Copy by Peter Bruegel the Younger)*
(1566) Tempera and oil on wood panel, 70 x 100 cm.

117. PEASANT BRAWL *(School of P. P. Rubens) Gouache, 25.7 × 37.1 cm.*

118. THE ROBBERS *(1565?) (Copy by Peter Brueghel the Younger) Oil on wood panel, 35 × 47.5 cm.*

119. THE LAND OF PLENTY (1567) Oil on wood panel. 52 × 78 cm.

120. THE BIRD'S-NESTER *(1568) Oil on wood panel, 59 × 68 cm.*

dye ten neſt Weet dye Weeten
dyen Roſt die heeten

121. **THE BEEKEEPERS** *(about 1569) Ink drawing, 20.3 × 30.9 cm.*

122. THE CRIPPLES *(1569) Oil on wood panel, 18 × 21 cm.*

Ou dat de Werelt is soe ongetru
Daer om gha ic in den ru

123. THE MISANTHROPIST *(1568) Tempera on canvas, 85 × 85 cm.*

124. THE PARABLE OF THE BLIND *(1568) Tempera on canvas, 86 × 154 cm.*

125.

125–129. THE PARABLE OF THE BLIND *Details: the blind men.*

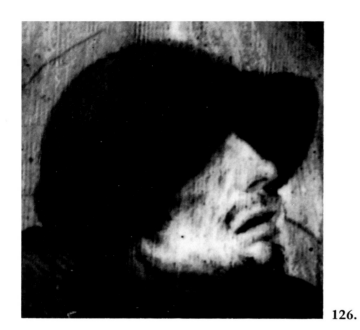

126.

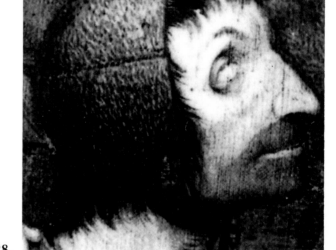

128.

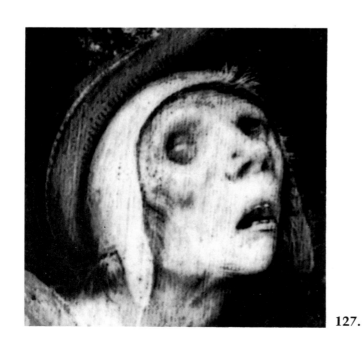

127.

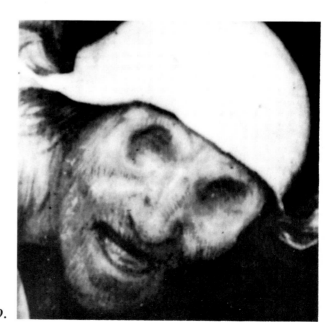

129.

VII. – The Outcome

It may not be all that surprising that the *naer het leeven* drawings (so called because each one is inscribed with these Flemish words meaning "from life") should so long have been attributed to Bruegel. It seemed plausible enough, after all. We have the testimony of van Mander who declared that Bruegel "handled the pen with a great deal of precision when sketching figures *from life*," and surely these drawings of men and women so carefully observed in the marketplace or on the street had to be the ones he had in mind. One might well have wondered, nonetheless, at the fact that Bruegel's line should be so different in these drawings, so much heavier and slower than in all the others. Strange, too, as I noted in the French edition of this book, that "with one possible exception, none of these figures should have found its way into the paintings." And indeed, a recent and more thoughtful examination (by Joaneath Spicer) has removed the whole body of these drawings from Bruegel's work and definitely attributed them to Roelant Savery.

Bruegel himself must have turned out drawings in the same vein; there is no special reason to doubt van Mander's account on this point. However, we can only speculate as to their number and appearance and deplore that not one of them has survived. Of course, the paintings are in very much the same key when they present one with a mass of little figures, some reduced to two legs sticking out from under a cape and wearing headgear in the shape of an iron salad bowl or a felt lampshade that swallows up the head entirely. There can be no doubt that Bruegel had actually seen all of these figures. Each has an inner life even though its depiction may still be quite rudimentary, finding expression in the stance and the movement of the body, as it stands evoked by the free play of the artist's brush. The subtle psychological conflicts and contradictions, which Rembrandt, for in-

The Way to Calvary
(detail, 1564)

stance, was to reveal in his portrayal of a single man, are rendered here through the teeming diversity of Bruegel's crowds. This is also what makes the presence of a large number of figures so significant in his work. Consider, for instance, the man who teases a child by swiping his cap and holding it just out of reach above his head. This vignette would certainly not strike one the same way if Bruegel had not placed it in the vicinity of the circle of onlookers surrounding Calvary. Each single body, caught in the crowd with its significant dress, is like a sign or cipher, and the sum of all these bodies presents the viewer with the expressive and entirely plausible features not of any single individual but of humankind collectively confronted with its fate.

I have attempted to show that Bruegel sought to present this fate as a drama. This drama could be that of meaning as it is unfolded in his religious works, or it could be the drama and the enigma of nature viewed as a presence and a process in his landscapes. It is for this reason that individual faces had not been all that important in his work up to now—with the single exception of *The Adoration of the Magi* of 1564. He may occasionally show a close-up of a man or a woman, but then the face appears quite round and undefined, so that one is not even tempted to pause to consider it. *The Land of Milk and Honey* is an example of this, as is *The Bird's-nester*. Bruegel, throughout his life, remained a distanced observer. His distance, however, was an unusual compound of lucidity, sympathy, reserve, irony, and humor. It was perhaps this same distance that led him, when he finally tried his hand at a real portrait, to paint the faces of blind men—faces, in other words, that he could consider at leisure, as though they were no more than a semantic object, a form deprived of the single central feature of any portrait in the usual sense: the attentive gaze and the inner presence it communicates.

It seems, then, that Bruegel began to take a more sustained interest in the portrait, or at least in the human face at this point. But since he was, first and foremost, a

Roelant Savery, Peasant Woman from the *Naer het leven* series, formerly attributed to Peter Bruegel.

lover of the dapple, kaleidoscopic aspect of life and of all human activity, this led him, in his last works, to attempt an entirely novel synthesis of the rowdy celebration and the portrait, of the popular and the heroic, in which he never quite renounced his inclination to see all his subjects as "types." He was never really drawn to the aspect of an individual taken by and in himself. What did attract him was the individual, any individual, insofar as he was involved with others and with the web of his world and age. Bruegel's quite exceptional powers shine forth in the way he rendered all this in a down-to-earth idiom that seems entirely *natural* to the spectator.

The last three paintings Bruegel produced provide a final synthesis of his reflections—a final statement that can be taken as a satisfying, if premature, conclusion to his lifework. In the second series of religious works as well as in the allegorical and proverbial sequence, I examined in chapter VI, Bruegel dealt with the inhumanity and "folly" that are the more despairing aspects of all history. Both lines of reflection appeared to lead the artist up a philosophical dead end. The model afforded by *The Conversion of Saint Paul* could only be considered a symbolic one, whereas *The Parable of the Blind* seems to suggest that "none is so blind as the one who will not see"—and to project the moral blindness this concept implies on society (*de werelt soe ongetru*) in general. But then, in 1568, a painting in quite different mood appears to offer Bruegel's final response to every cheap and unimaginative form of pessimism. The context in which *The Magpie on the Gallows* was painted was both politically and morally a gloomy one, and this lends even greater force to the work's emotional content. The painting is a landscape—world encompassing, splendid, diverse, and flooded with light. One can make out a mill, a small town, a fortified castle, a broad plain, a river, and, beyond it, mountains and the sea . . . , but also, full center, on the very spot that in the past had been reserved for the allegorical figure ("Mad Meg," for instance) the gallows stands, a familiar and disquieting personage, arrogantly poised there on bandy legs. Somewhat farther down the slope, and facing it as though they were engaged in an endless and wordless conversation, is a wooden cross. No body hangs from the gallows; no figure of Christ, from the cross. And, one may wonder, what can these two instruments of execution, one the tool of justice, the other, it is said, of love, find to tell one another? What is the substance of the debate they are fated to pursue until the end of time?

But then, as though to interrupt all such solemn thoughts, two garrulous magpies butt in with their habitual insolence. One of them has settled on a stump, the other is perched atop the gallows. As in the foreground of *The Way to Calvary*, a horse's skull lies at the foot of the mound, possibly a reminiscence of the human skull that, in medieval imagery, is placed at the base of the cross to signify its victory over death.

A detail on the lower left-hand corner is quite typical of the traits that sometimes caused Bruegel to be considered "vulgar" in the past. A man has taken down his trousers and is relieving himself at the foot of the gallows. If Bruegel placed him there, it was not just in order to indulge in some facile anal humor. The naturalistic detail plays a symbolic role that has always been fully understood in popular parlance, though psychology only turned its attention to it in the present century.[1] For this, in view of the location, can be seen as the universal and instinctive way of thumbing one's nose at death, repression, and at all the hardships of human existence and of asserting that, in spite of all this, *there is life.*

Further off, in a clearing beyond the gallows, a small troop of men and women have come up from the town together with a bagpipe player. They are shown dancing beneath the gallows with inexhaustible élan and a joy that even the grim presence of the gallows cannot extinguish. It is the dancers who light up this world with their resolute cheer as it shines forth beneath the delicate foliage of the surrounding trees. The world about them once more unfolds in the full breadth that Bruegel gave it in the past. For if the gallows does indeed "stand at the heart of every joy" (as the poet Erich Arendt declares, in referring to this painting), it cannot quell the delight of men. Instead, it lends it a greater and more poignant intensity. As all these dancing figures appear to suggest, a joy of such quality is only possible to the extent that the "gallows" *has* indeed found its place, to the extent that all that is negative and incomplete in respect to the desires of all men has been acknowledged, accepted, and transcended. For it must be acknowledged—not with the thought that it will ultimately be erased and forgotten in the life to come (thus canceling out the inherent and obvious contradictions of the present world), but rather, and in the absence of any solution that may yet be conveniently expressed, quite simply accepted as a fact of this nether world and of nature, so that a deep and human joy may flame forth nonetheless. This then is Bruegel's last response to the capital question that the allegorical figure of death raised early on in his lifework. And this response expresses both a solution and a resolution that henceforth seem to carry the artist with them like a tide until he shortly reaches his end. Such notions can quite easily be expressed in these terms today, but this does not mean that Bruegel himself could have put them into words. Quite to the contrary, he always expressed himself as poets do, in other words as does a man who *speaks more things than he himself clearly knows.* His art anticipates, through relationships that are made plainly perceptible by his brushstrokes, concepts that would still require several centuries to mature. This demonstrates the manner in which art manages to anticipate and open up ways, not by the intervention of some divine or prophetic grace, but because this really is the way things normally and naturally unfold. Every reality is only gradually raised to a level at which it can be clearly perceived and expressed. It is at first grasped only through a groping intuition, felt through the roots of

---

[1] See *The Flemish Proverbs* (il. 32), the man with his bare behind hanging out of the window to the right.

one's being, tangible and yet unutterable for the simple reason that the very words by which it might be uttered have not yet been forged.[2]

It can be felt even before it is actually noticed. For *to notice* something is, at first, to cast it off into the distance. Only then, once this distance has been established, does it become possible to see it, to name it, to give it a face and a concept, to welcome it, to embrace it, and to bring it into the communal reality of language. All this is being accomplished in this very moment, night and day, as it has unceasingly been accomplished, ever since the dawn of human time, at every level of society. The artist, however, has a peculiar ability that allows him to lend a shape and an appearance to such latent realities, even as they still lie sleeping in the antechamber of our awareness.

This, then, is why Bruegel's art strikes us as so familiar. And this also accounts, in part, for the failure of those who later set out to copy his work. For they could not perceive, in the reality of the world, all the things that Bruegel had observed and painted and that belonged, quite beyond any form that can be squared and copied on canvas, to the "immaterial" realm of human intentions and relationships. *Multa pingit quae pingi non possunt,* said Ortels: "He painted many things that cannot be painted." And they cannot be painted *as such* because they belong to the realm, not so much of the invisible as of the *unseen*: the subtle, expressive domain whose messages are perceived, even though the messenger goes unnoticed.

It has been suggested, but never really established, that Bruegel was of peasant stock. If van Mander is not mistaken, he must have lived, for some time at least, in his native village. That is as far as we can go—and even this much is unsure. It is quite apparent, of course, that he felt at ease in a rustic environment and that he was familiar with the proper etiquette of peasant societies. But then again, he seems to have gone there as an observer, and not in order to seek out a climate that he missed because he was living in a town. His love for a serving girl does not signify much either. Goethe, bourgeois genius and statesman that he was, married a woman of low extraction. In any event, Bruegel, once he had reached his full maturity and the mastery of his art, should be regarded as a humanist of great scope, and if he ultimately turned his attention to the peasants, it may well be that he found in them a universal truth—a truth that appeared to him during his rural childhood, a deep, tenacious, and to him essential vision whose formulation, as he saw it, could only be reached by referring to these peasant bodies and faces.

Two large "peasant paintings" of this period are undated, but it seems likely that Bruegel painted them in 1569. Later on an anonymous artisan added 5.5 cm to the bottom of *The Wedding Feast* to make it the same size as *The Peasant Dance*. In both works Bruegel once again forsakes the high prospect he formerly favored and places himself at the same level as the scene he chooses to paint. The wedding feast is being held in a barn and about forty people are present. Some are seated on either side of the long table, others are shoving and jostling one another to get in through the barn door. The bride, with her hair down as custom demanded, is certainly no beauty. She sits there quite absorbed within herself, hands joined and momentarily unaware of what is going on around her. The groom is most likely the man, dressed in black, pouring drinks in the foreground, for he is required (by custom once again) to serve the guests at his own wedding. Two pipers have been hired to provide the necessary festive din. One of them has just paused, however, and can be seen observing the arrival of the food with a dreamy, indeed almost a pleading look. The plates he is ogling have been laid out on a door that, for the occasion, has been turned into a tray. The lord of the manor, seated on the right, is engaged in conversation with a monk. His greyhound's elegant muzzle emerges from under the table. In the foreground, meanwhile, a little girl with well-buttered chops sits on the ground sucking her fingers and polishing off her dish. Except for the piper suffering from hunger pangs, everybody appears quite concentrated on the business at hand.

And that business is food. The subject of the painting is food. It is food we see in the foreground, focusing the attention of the guests, and it is to partake of it that people are jostling one another in the background, near the door. The diagonal perspective sets the accent upon the path taken by food and drink, starting with the groom filling up the pots in the foreground, and moving down the table toward the people who can be seen emptying them in the background. The entrance of the food is also made conspicuous by the composition. Hands stretch out to seize it as it passes by, to place it on the board before which each guest is solemnly engaged in eating. For feasting is a serious occupation when abundance is never assured. Bruegel certainly does not indulge in the characteristic absurdities of Flemish baroque. His meal is deeply ceremonious. The guests are mindful to honor this abundance, to take three helpings of each dish, even if they are no longer hungry, so that the body may remember this day and that the memory may honor the bridal pair.[3]

The *Peasant Dance*, by contrast, is taking place outdoors, on the village green. Here the piper's mind is on his business. Cheeks inflated like balloons from years of blowing into his instrument, he is working hard for his pay. His shrewd little eyes reveal this, but he is also enjoying himself, and the dancers will get their money's worth. The piper, here, is an embodiment of the music that sets the world in motion. A young peasant, seated beside him, gawks and listens in rapt attention. The

[2] See, for instance, Lucien Fèbvre, *Le Problème de l'Incroyance au XVIe siècle* (The Problem of Unbelief in the Sixteenth Century), Albin Michel, Paris, p. 328 "Les Mots qui manquent" (The Missing Words).

[3] In Rabelais' country, in those days, guests sought to impress the date of weddings on their memory by giving one another a cheerful drubbing (See *Le Quart Livre,* chapter 14).

dance has just begun, and the couples come running up from left and right. Toward the rear, dressed in red and yellow cloth, the indispensable fool encourages the dancers, but he is no longer allowed to assume the didactic stance he took in former works.

Behind the piper stands a table where people sit and drink. They drink at first to ease the flow of words. Arms outstretched, they grasp for terms they cannot find. The fellow in the middle has already reached a point at which everything looks blurred. The words come pouring out of his mouth, but he no longer seems to know why. Yet he has clearly managed to catch one woman's fancy, and she thrusts her lumpy, gluttonous face towards him, begging a kiss like the one being exchanged by the couple standing behind her. As the crown of leaves on its roof proclaims, the house on the left is a tavern. A man in the doorway empties his mug while another one voids his bladder with his nose to the wall. The dancers, meanwhile, are lifted up with a resolute élan, carried away by a pugnacious delight that lends a sudden lightness to their heavy features.

These two paintings may need going over in this way at first, but their deeper coherence does not depend on any simple narrative procedure. The real narrative makes itself understood through a composition and an interplay of color so straightforward that they may escape notice. Yet these paintings, in their apparent simplicity, are the end result of over twenty years of artistic experience. The attitudes shown here must also have been observed "from life," but they have acquired heroic proportions that Bruegel undoubtedly borrowed from the Italian style, though he endowed them with a new significance. Michelangelo's bodies present one with a titanic and rather overwhelming model. One is reminded of Sigmund Freud subjugated by his statue of Moses. Bruegel adopted these same imposing proportions (though without excess) to lend a density and a grandeur to these peasants who stand, like the last, and no doubt the most impenetrable representation, in his interrupted work, of the anonymity (or "incognito") of the light. These gross and simple people, whose features, now that they are at last fully defined, do not seem at all beautiful (as are all those who populate Italian paintings), stood, in Bruegel's sight, for the ultimate personification of life's own courage and determination. He did not choose to paint them to confirm some wealthy burgher in the sense of his own superiority—that would, all too often, be the undertaking of the generations of painters that were to follow. Bruegel,

instead and through their mediation, revealed life gushing forth at its very source: vigorous, canny, direct, innocent in its impulses, and above all tenacious, incorrigibly tenacious.

The profound and original vision that Bruegel proposed would subsequently be imitated only in its most outward manifestations. There is a quality to Bruegel, an intuitive perception of the intentions that the visible world of man manages to express through each gesture, attitude, and object, and that is only encountered with a comparable intensity (and likewise without any apparent esthetic derivation) in the work of Honoré Daumier. Other painters, since Bruegel's time, have shown us scenes of daily life and its everyday objects. They may, like Jan Vermeer, have sought to capture a moment of silence and suspended time. They may, like Jacob Jordaens, have bellowed their implausible devotion to carnality and drink. But from this time on, things begin to be viewed in a more bourgeois perspective. The object begins to elude the power of those who live with it until it is gradually turned into an object of veneration.

No object had this transcendent value of the fetish in Bruegel's sight. Things found their meaning in the use one made of them. Each object appears in his work as the trace of an individual activity and a practical initiative. Each gesture and attitude, each piece of clothing, each tool, all industry, all work, each one of the objects in common use that Bruegel happened to paint, and even the broken jug handle lying in the dust under the dancers' feet, clearly referred beyond themselves to the craft and labor that produced them. And in doing so they became the tangible sign of a pursuit, of an unending search that, through the hand, heart, and mind of man, is that ventured from age to age, innovative and vital, by all human dissatisfaction and desire.

Bruegel completed at least one more painting—though it has now been lost. It was entitled *The Moment When Truth Breaks Out.* According to van Mander, Bruegel considered this his most accomplished work. But perhaps we should not grieve too much at its loss. The painter of *The Fall of Icarus* himself might well have found this in keeping with his own warm-hearted irony. Today, the title of the work alone is known while the painting itself, the very painting that presumably revealed that ultimate epiphany of meaning or unmeaning that Bruegel's entire work had always been striving after, has finally been all but forgotten and has vanished without a trace.

130. THE WEDDING FEAST *Detail: the tray bearer.*

131. **THE WEDDING FEAST** *(1568–69) Oil on wood panel, 114 × 163 cm.*

132. THE WEDDING FEAST *Detail: the crowd beside the door.*

133. **THE WEDDING FEAST** *Detail: the little girl.*

134. **THE PEASANT DANCE** *Detail: the table.*

135. **THE PEASANT DANCE** *Detail: dancing couple.*

136. THE PEASANT DANCE *(1568) Oil on wood panel, 114 × 164 cm.*

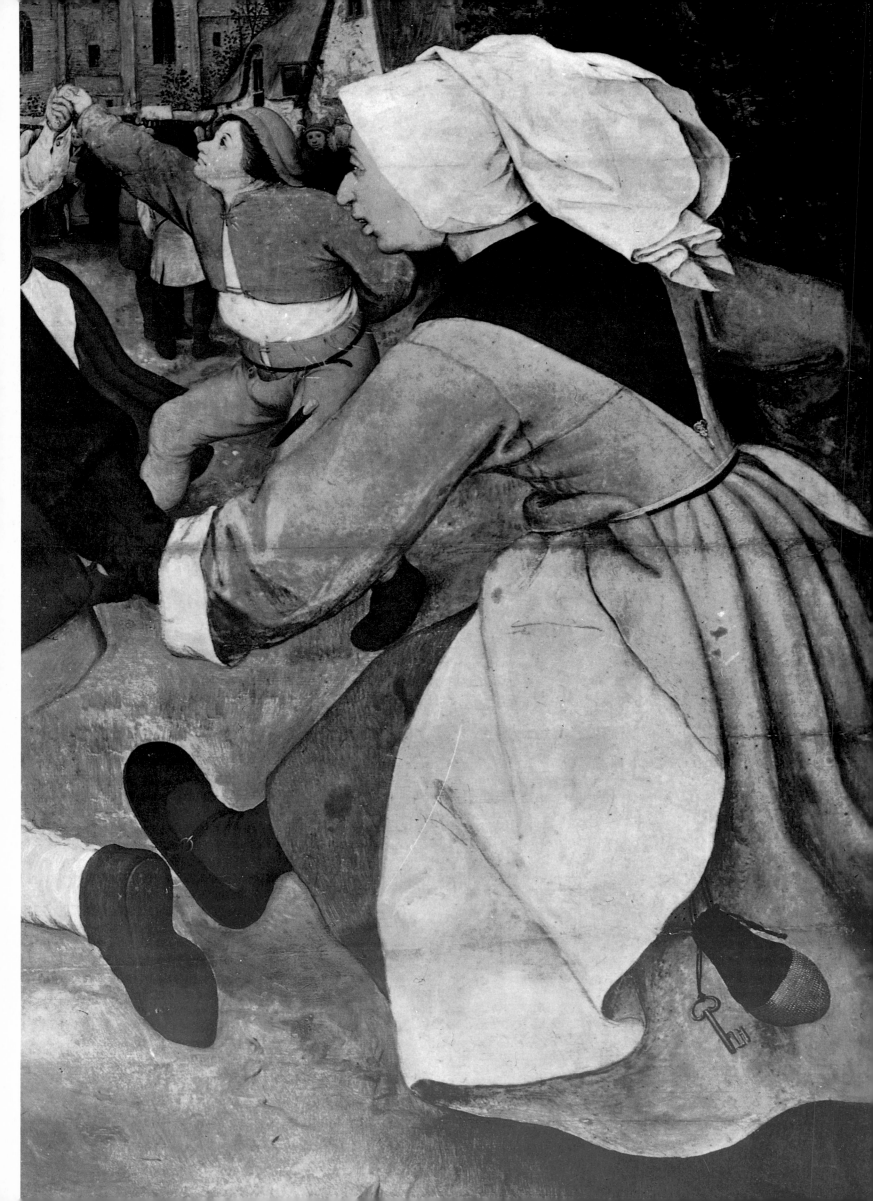

138. **THE MAGPIE ON THE GALLOWS** *(1568) Oil on wood panel.*

139. **THE MAGPIE ON THE GALLOWS** *Detail.*
(See overleaf)

137. **THE PEASANT DANCE** *Detail: dancing woman.*

140. *Joost de Momper* THE TEMPEST *(Formerly attributed to P. Bruegel.) Oil on wood panel, 70.5 × 97 cm.*

VIII. – The Heritage

Bruegel had two sons, Peter and Jan, as well as numerous imitators. But can any of these be considered his heirs? Should one not say rather, that his inheritance was scattered and squandered?

His own children did not learn anything from Bruegel. Peter was only five when his father died, and Jan was barely one. As for their sister Marie, the date of her birth remains unrecorded, but, in any event, she did not become an artist. Maryken, Bruegel's widow, had her husband buried in the church of Notre Dame de la Chapelle where they had been married six years before. Nine years later she would be buried there beside him, having barely reached her thirties. At that point the children were taken under the wing of their energetic grandmother; young Peter was then fourteen, and Jan, ten. She took them with her and returned to Antwerp in the year following the sack of the town and the massacre of its inhabitants by mercenaries without pay—the lost children whom Alva had left behind him when he departed.

In Antwerp, Peter, having reached the requisite age, was put in apprenticeship with a painter. Van Mander says it was Gillis van Coninxloo. An uncertainty arises on this point, however, for three artists with this name lived in Antwerp at the time. Van Mander assumed it was the landscape painter of repute, for he had never heard of the other two. Georges Marlier, however, in his imposing posthumous work on Peter Brueghel the Younger, reveals the existence of a second Gillis van Coninxloo, and then a third, the latter's father. Now this father (please bear with me) had married the widow of Peter Coeck van Aelst's brother and was thus related, after a fashion, to the three Brueghel children and to their tutelary grandmother.

Must we then assume that Peter was conveniently placed as an apprentice with this vague relative? After having cast doubt upon former certainties, Marlier does not really make a definite pronouncement, but he does seem to favor van Mander's version. Let us then assume, with all appropriate hedging, that the young boy was indeed apprenticed to the landscape painter. This would allow for just five years of apprenticeship, since, as a result of events that will be mentioned in due course, Peter's master left Antwerp in 1585 and moved to Frankenthal in Germany. That same year Peter was registered, like his father, at the Guild of Saint Luke, but whereas his father had been received as a full-fledged master, the son was registered as "Peeter Brugel, master's son." He was thus given the benefit of a rule that dispensed with the obligation of a master's son being registered as a pupil and thus having to pay the fee this required. The rule implied that a master's son would be trained in his father's workshop, which could obviously not be the case with young Peter.

So what had happened in 1585? That year had been a particularly painful for the city of Antwerp, and the events that occurred then had some drastic consequences. Flanders had, for many years, been a battlefield on which the armies of various parties and countries clashed. The countryside was ruined, sacked, flooded, deserted. William of Orange—William the Silent—still pursued his war against the Spaniards, and the city of Antwerp happened to be in no-man's-land. It was thus subject to constant changes of government that alternated according to the fortunes of war, as the Catholics and then the Calvinists gained the upper hand. At one point a French army also decided to try its luck and capture the wealthy merchant city. In 1583, François of Anjou took Antwerp and entered the city. But then, quite unexpectedly, the cautious burghers went berserk. It was bad enough, it seems, to have the Spaniards perpetually on one's back, but the coming of the French was the last straw—a total stranger mixing into what had become a family quarrel. The French troops probably behaved no worse than had all the others. In any event the exasperated burghers took up arms, attacked the enemy that had already settled in, and slaughtered every one of them.

But the people of Antwerp had barely rid themselves of the French when another army stood before their gates: This time they were Spaniards and Italians, commanded by Alexander Farnese. This general had brought Ghent around to Philip II in 1584. Brussels, and then Antwerp, would surrender in 1585. Thus did the great crisis, which had ravaged the Netherlands for close to twenty years, come to an end.

The war had been waged for the domination of a rich merchant city and its port where trading ships sailed in to unload wares from all over the world. By the end of the conflict, Antwerp had become a mere shadow of its former self. The Protestant burghers naturally went into exile. But they were by no means the only ones to leave. William of Orange had placed a permanent blockade on the Scheld, which had, in the long run, consummated the ruin of the port. People gradually left the city in which all trade had been paralyzed. The artists, such as Gillis van Coninxloo, emigrated, in search of wealthier societies that could afford their services. The intellectuals left in hopes of finding a more liberal climate elsewhere.

The exodus of Flemish painters served to propagate the style and subject matter of Flemish art throughout Europe. The Brueghels, however, remained in Antwerp. One may assume that the two boys, who were not yet full-fledged masters, had not been offered an opportunity to work outside the city.

Jan began his apprenticeship at the age of fourteen—in the very year that the French were slaughtered in the burghers' uprising. His grandmother had placed him with

Anthony van Dyck,
Portrait of Peter Brueghel
the Younger.

a painter and dealer named Peter Goetkint. But Goetkint died the following year, and Marlier supposes that Jan thereafter studied with his grandmother, Mayken Verhulst Coeck. She had, it is believed, already taught the craft of distemper painting to Peter the Elder when he was her husband's apprentice.

There is not much ready information touching upon the career of the two sons. Peter produced abundantly—mostly copies of his father's work. He had a number of pupils, but only two of these are still known today: Fransken Snyders, an animal and still-life painter, and Gonzales Coques, a painter of portraits and interiors. Despite the abundance of his production and his long career, Peter did not grow wealthy. He died in the course of the academic year 1637–1638. Shortly thereafter Elizabeth Goddelet, his widow, also died. An excellent engraved portrait of Peter the Younger by Anthony van Dyck shows a man in his sixties with a sorrowful and weary face.

Somewhat more is known about Jan. He left Antwerp upon reaching his majority and traveled to Italy by way of Cologne. He was in Naples in 1590 (he was then twenty-two), in Rome in 1593 and 1594. There he met Cardinal Federigo Borromeo who brought him to Milan the following year. Jan returned to Antwerp after spending a year and a half in the service of the cardinal and enrolled in the Guild of Saint Luke. He traveled in Germany and Bohemia, became the court painter of Archduke Albert and Archduchess Isabella after they had been appointed to govern the southern Netherlands (Belgium) in 1599. These new rulers strove to restore order and prosperity. Jan amassed a considerable fortune and became dean of the painters' guild. He was a friend and collaborator of Rubens (from whom he commissioned a painting for the monument that he had placed on his parents' tomb), and he was active in several professional and social groups, including the Chamber of Rhetoric (the Stock-flower) of which several of his father's friends had been members. He died in January 1625, carried off, along with three of his ten children, by a cholera epidemic. We know that he inherited his father's painting *Christ and the Adulterous Woman.* He bequeathed it, in his will, to Cardinal Borromeo, and six months after his death, the painting was sent to Italy. The cardinal, however, was unwilling to keep it. He had a copy made (the

one in the Bergamo museum?) and thoughtfully returned it to Jan the Younger, the son of his former protégé.

A certain confusion arises out of the fact that reference is occasionally made to a "Velvet Brueghel" and to a "Hell Brueghel." The "Velvet" nickname undoubtedly designates Jan and came, according to Hulin de Loo, "from the habit he had of wearing velvet clothing". Another author (Marlier) quotes this hypothesis but goes on to wonder whether the name did not refer to "the velvety surface of his precious little paintings."

As for the "Hell Brueghel," Hulin asserts that this was also Jan and that the name referred to the "fires and infernos, usually with mythological subjects, that he often painted, especially in his youth." The explanation appears satisfactory, especially since Peter the Younger never painted subjects of this kind. But it seems to be the business of historians to reduce satisfactory explanations to rubble. Marlier made a scrupulous study of all the inventories of seventeenth-century collections in which the names of the Brueghel brothers or of their father appear. He concludes that, even as early as 1614, when "he still had a quarter of a century to live," Peter the Younger was already known as "Hell Brueghel." This would confirm the opinion of a number of authors who had always been convinced of the fact, but who had consequently attributed to Peter the Younger a good number of little "hell" paintings that had actually been painted by Jan.

What appears clear today is that "Velvet Brueghel" refers to Jan, and "Hell Brueghel," to Peter—despite the fact that all the little infernal visions were, in fact, painted by the former.

Both artists copied their father's works, but Peter turned the undertaking into an industry. *The Preaching of John the Baptist,* for instance, was copied twenty-three times by Peter and his workshop (three times by Jan), and *Adoration of the Magi in Winter* exists in twenty-eight versions, all of them by Peter or his workshop. The same thing holds true of a number of other works by Bruegel the Elder. Copies were made of works that still exist today but also of others whose former existence is only attested by the surviving copy.

One is naturally led to wonder how the sons could have known works by their father that had been sold and scattered abroad long before either of them had been born. All the copies, and even those of Peter the Younger, despite their obvious weaknesses, appear remarkably faithful to the original. The father's strong passion and compassion, his psychological and spiritual insight are lacking in most of them. Everything is accurate enough, but like a wax museum effigy, the missing element is the actual impression of life. "One may well wonder," Marlier concludes, "whether the sons might not have used a counterdrawing. This would account for the fact that not only the scale but even the drawing, down to the smallest detail, is identical, and that the only differences one encounters is in the use of certain colors. . . ."

The production of copies of Bruegel the Elder seems to account for the major part of Peter's output, and he definitely appears to be the less original and less gifted of the two brothers. But his copies are also uneven in quality, and he may often have signed inferior versions produced by his assistants. No doubt, his chief merit is that he worked to increase his father's reputation at a time when the art book did not yet exist.

His original works, of which about forty are known today, are not without a certain naïve charm. They depict rustic scenes, rural celebrations, and village fairs with their stock characters. They are pretty, picturesque, and devoid both of pretention and of imagination. It seems rather unfair, in fact, to compare the son with his father. Peter the Younger had none of the Elder's scope, but he did have certain qualities of his own, and the comparison can only be justified when it concerns a copy of one of his father's works. One may, in fact, suppose that had he not been saddled with that cumbersome heritage, Peter the Younger might have painted in a quite different style, or might even have chosen some other profession than that of dynastic heir. This is what one seems to read in the melancholy gaze recorded by van Dyck—a melancholy quite opposed to the easygoing mood encountered in his paintings.

Jan's case is quite different. Peter was five when his father died. One can well imagine the gap this left in his existence and the need he must have felt to bring his father back to life by churning out countless paintings in his manner. Jan, on the other hand, never even knew his father. His temper was more mobile and independent than that of Peter's. His vitality and his imagination, too, were quite his own. He always remained distinctly Flemish in his idiom, but he traveled all over Europe, went to Italy, steeped himself in the mood of the baroque, and while remaining his father's son in many perceptible ways, he finally managed to assimilate his inheritance and to produce an entirely original body of work—full of dapple color, vitality, imagination, and sensitivity. His production was abundant and dealt with a wide range of subjects: little "hell" paintings, allegories, biblical and historical scenes, genre paintings, still lifes, animal paintings, and also the big, luminous, and varied bouquets of flowers that are so typical of his work.

The comparison between the two brothers offers a paradigm of the problem inherent to any heritage. Peter apparently wished to contribute to the survival and propagation of his father's work. But he tried to ensure it by means of a merely external and formal imitation that suggests a much too rigid fixation on an utterly vanished past. Jan, on the other hand, since he never suffered from such a fixation, felt free to use some traits inherited from his father (and that his grandmother may have handed on to him) while fixing them freely with other influences. And he used all of them to serve his own view of things, a view that is full of the vitality and cheer so typical of the father too, but that appear in Jan's work in the new form the new age required. The father, we may assume, was a man who had emerged from relatively modest social circumstances (even if he was not of peasant stock), and who generally preferred the company of intellectuals and cultivated townsmen. Jan, benefiting from his father's credit, found himself at ease in an aristocratic

Anthony van Dyck,
Portrait of Jan Brueghel

society and was familiar with the great. His dealings with Cardinal Borromeo must have been quite strongly marked with friendship, considering that he willed a painting to the Italian prelate. His friendship and long collaboration with Rubens also placed him at the center of a cosmopolitan society, and his ties with the archduke and archduchess made his social situation quite different from that of his father. His paintings are precious and picturesque and swarming with details, and they reflect an awareness of a new social project—the Counter-Reformation, of which Rubens was the most visible spokesman in the realm of the arts.

Nature seen as a power and a presence, and man considered as a philosophical problem—the central issues of the father's painting—are not to be found in Jan's work.

Jan's view of man is that of a city dweller. He had become a true bourgeois, and he no longer had that keen practical awareness of the demanding activity inherent in any physical labor that is so apparent in the work of the Elder Bruegel. Jan's characters parade about in their finest clothes. They travel. Such are the reasonable activities of people engaged in trade. Other men can be seen handling the merchandise, loading and unloading it, but Jan is unconcerned by the effort this implies and gives it no more thought than would a traveler who entrusts his luggage to a porter. This is apparent in the treatment of the bodies in his paintings. A cursory glance might not find a great difference between his crowds and those of his father, but as soon as one takes a closer look, a difference does indeed become apparent. Bruegel the Elder always seemed to delve beneath the show to see what forces are at work there. Jan, on the other hand, was pleased to savor the world in its diversity. He was a painter, not a thinker. He had a painter's eye and an analytic visual intelligence. He delighted in color; he loved the light and the iridescent remoteness of landscape. He also had a certain sociable warmth that was the basis of his ease in society and allowed him to accept the world as it was. He did not aspire to be a thinker as his father had been, but his temper and his intelligence, together with the attractive freshness of his talent, allowed him to be a competent servant of the new doctrine of his day.

141. *Peter Brueghel the Younger,* MASSACRE OF THE
INNOCENTS *(1604) Oil on wood panel, 120 × 167 cm.*

142. *Peter Brueghel the Younger,* PEASANT DANCE OUT
OF DOORS *Oil on wood panel, 77 × 160 cm.*

143. *Peter Brueghel the Younger,* THE PREACHING OF SAINT
JOHN THE BAPTIST *(1565) Oil on wood panel, 95 × 160 cm.*

144. *Peter Brueghel the Younger,* THE PREACHING OF SAINT
JOHN THE BAPTIST *Oil on wood panel, 119 × 167 cm.*

145. *Peter Brueghel the Younger,* THE CRUCI-
FIXION *Oil on wood panel, 150 × 192 cm.*

146. *Peter Brueghel the Younger,* PEASANTS AT TABLE
OUT OF DOORS *Oil on wood panel, 37 × 61 cm.*

147. *Jan Brueghel,* THE PREACHING OF JOHN THE BAPTIST
(1598) Oil on wood panel, 41 × 59 cm.

148. *Peter Brueghel the Younger or Jan Brueghel,* CHRIST AND THE
ADULTEROUS WOMAN *Grisaille on wood panel, 24 × 31 cm.*

149. *Jan Brueghel,* JONAH CAST UP BY THE WHALE *(toward
1595–1596) Oil on wood panel, 37.5 × 55.6 cm.*

150. *Jan Brueghel,* ROAD THROUGH THE WOODS *Oil on
wood panel, 25 × 38 cm.*

151. *Jan Brueghel,* BOUQUET OF FLOWERS *Oil on wood panel,*
113 × 86 cm.

152. *Jan Brueghel,* CHRIST PREACHING IN A PORT
(1598) *Oil on wood panel, 78 × 119 cm.*

153. *Jan Brueghel,* THE BATTLE OF ARBELLES
(or of IXUS) *(1602) Oil on wood panel, 36
× 80 cm. Musée du Louvre, Paris.*

154. Jan Brueghel THE EARTHLY PARADISE.

155. Jan Brueghel THE EARTHLY PARADISE WITH
ADAM AND EVE *(about 1616) Oil on wood
panel, 74 × 114 cm.*

156. Jan Brueghel (scenery) and P. P. Rubens (figures),
ALLEGORY OF HEARING *(1617–1618) Oil on
wood panel, 65 × 101 cm.*

174

Chronology of Peter Bruegel's Life and Works

1525 Presumed date of Peter Bruegel's birth, in Bruegel (or Brögel), near Breda in the northern part of Brabant.

1550 Bruegel may have entered the workshop of Peter Balten after the death of Peter Coeck van Aelst, his first teacher. Emperor Charles V sent down the "placards" (edicts) against the heretics.

1551 Bruegel registers as a master in the Guild of Saint Luke in Antwerp.

1552 Bruegel travels to Italy, passing through France (Lyon). On his way to Sicily (Messina, Palermo?), he may have witnessed the burning of Reggio di Calabria by the Turks.
Drawing: Mountain Landscape with an Italian-style Cloister (il. 82).

1553 Heading north, he visits Naples, Rome (befriending the miniaturist Julio Clovio), and Bologna (meeting the geographer Scipio Fabius). In Rome sees paintings by Michelangelo and Raphael.
Drawings: Landscape with Town and Saint Jerome (no il.); various mountain landscapes including the "large Rhine landscape" (no il.); Landscape with Walled Town (il. 83); Alpine Landscape (il. 84).
Paintings: Landscape with Christ Appearing to the Apostles (no il.). View of the Saint Gothard Pass (lost painting that belonged to P. P. Rubens).

1554 Probable date of his return to Antwerp by way of the Alps and the Rhine valley.
Drawings: Six further mountain landscapes (no il.).

1555 *Drawings:* Four other mountain landscapes (no il.); Alpine Landscape with Two Mules (il. 85); Alpine Landscape with an Artist Sketching (il. 86).

1556 Goes to work for Jerome Cock, printmaker at The Sign of the Four Winds. Bruegel is influenced by Cock, a great admirer of Hieronymous Bosch. Plague and famine occur in Brussels.
Drawings: Two Mountain Landscapes (no il.); The Temptation of Saint Anthony (il. 6); Big Fish Eat Little Fish (il. 7); The Ass at School (il. 8); The Seven Deadly Sins: Avarice (il. 14).
Paintings: The Epiphany (margin, p. 65).

1557 Associates with a circle of erudite and "libertine" (i.e., liberal) intellectuals in Antwerp: Ortels the geographer, Goltzius the archaeologist, Plantin the printer, Coornhert the religious thinker and engraver, and Franckert the art lover.
Drawings: The Seven Deadly Sins: Gluttony (il. 15), Lechery (il. 17), Wrath (il. 18), Envy (il. 19), Sloth (il. 20).
Engravings: Big Fish Eat Little Fish (no il.); The Ass at School (no il.).
Paintings: Landscape with the Parable of the Sower (margin, p. 39).

1558 Death of Charles V.
Drawings: The Alchemist (il. 9); Everyman (Elck) (il. 11); The Last Judgment (il. 21); The Skaters Before Saint George's Gate (il. 101).
Engravings: Alpine landscapes published by J. Cock (no il.); The Seven Deadly Sins (no il.); Everyman (Elck) (no il.); Penitent Mary Magdalene (il. 3); The Battle of the Safes and the Money Boxes (il. 5); The Alchemist (il. 10); Landscape with Saint Jerome (margin, p. 19).
Paintings: Yawning Man (no il.); View of the Port of Naples (margin, p. 15); Twelve Proverbs (margins, pp. 40 and 41).

1559 Marguerite of Parma appointed regent of the Netherlands. New "placards" issued by Philip II.
Drawings: The Kermess of Hoboken (il. 12); The Virtues: Faith (il. 22); Charity (il. 23); Prudence (il. 24); Hope (il. 25); Justice (il. 26); The Flight into Egypt (il. 65); View of Reggio During the Burning of the Town (il. 87).
Paintings: The Flemish Proverbs (il. 30, 31, 32); The Battle of Carnival and Lent (il. 38, 39).

1560 Begins to sign his work BRUEGEL instead of BRUEGHEL. (His sons reverted to the earlier spelling.) Granvelle, an admirer of Bruegel's works, is appointed Cardinal of Malines.
Drawings: The Virtues: Fortitude (il. 27), Temperance (il. 28).
Paintings: Children's Games (il. 34, 35, 36, 37).

1561 Scipio Fabius sends his greetings to Bruegel in a letter to Ortels. The Landjuweel (assembly of the Chambers of Rhetoric) is held in Antwerp. There is such license of language that the mayor is arrested and executed.
Drawings: Christ in Limbo (il. 2 and il. 29).

1562 Visits Amsterdam. From this year on, he devotes himself almost entirely to painting. Clandestine Calvinist meetings are held in Brussels.
Drawings: Two other views of Amsterdam (no il.); Three Blind Men (no il.); The Resurrection of Christ (il. 56); The Gates of Amsterdam (margin, p. 16).
Engravings: Warship prints (series continued until 1564) (no il.).
Paintings: Crazy Griet (Dulle Griet) (il. 44, 45, 46, 47); The Triumph of Death (il. 48, 49, 50, 51, 52, 53, 54, 55); The Fall of the Rebel Angels (il. 58); The Death of Saul (il. 66); Two Monkeys (margin, p. 67).

1563 Peter Bruegel weds Maryken Coeck, then aged about 20, the daughter of Peter Coeck van Aelst. They settle in Brussels.
Engravings: The Poor Kitchen (no il.); The Rich Kitchen (no il.); The Resurrection of Christ (il. 57).
Paintings: The (Smaller) Tower of Babel (il. 59); The (Larger) Tower of Babel (il. 60, 61, 62, 63); The Flight into Egypt (il. 64).

1564 Peter Brueghel the Younger is born. (Later, with his father dead, he apprenticed to a painter in Antwerp; he copied many of his father's paintings and was known as Hell Brueghel.)
Drawings: The Fall of the Magician (il. 13).
Paintings: The Death of the Virgin (il. 67); The Adoration of the Magi (il. 68, 69, 70, 71); The Way to Calvary (il. 72, 73, 74, 75, 76, 77, 78, 79, 80, 81); An Old Peasant Woman (margin, p. 119).

1565 Count Egmont goes to Spain to submit complaints about the Regent Council to the king. Scipio Fabius again writes to Ortels and mentions Bruegel. Jonghelink, a wealthy collector of Bruegel's work, offers 16 of the works as collateral.
Drawings: The Calumny of Apelles (no il.); The Painter and the Connoisseur (il. 1); Spring (il. 91).
Paintings: The Haymakers (il. 88, 89, 90); The Harvest (il. 92); Skaters with a Bird Trap (margin, p. 93); The Return of the Herd (il. 94, 95); The Dark Day (il. 96); The Hunters in the Snow (il. 98, 99); The Preaching of John the Baptist (il. 102, 103, 104); Christ and the Adulterous Woman (il. 105); The Unfaithful Shepherd (copy, il. 112); The Good Shepherd (copy, il. 113).

1566 The iconoclasts devastate 400 churches in the Netherlands.
Drawings: The Wedding of Mopsus and Nisa (il. 42).
Engravings: The Masquerade of Orson and Valentine (il. 41); Landscape with Rabbit Hunters (il. 100).
Paintings: The Massacre of the Innocents (il. 106); The Census in Bethlehem (il. 107).

1567 Guicciardini mentions Bruegel. The Duke of Alva enters Brussels with 60,000 Spanish soldiers.
Paintings: Adoration of the Magi in Winter (il. 108); The Conversion of Saint Paul (il. 110, 111); The Land of Plenty (il. 119).

1568 Jan Brueghel is born. (Jan became a painter of renown and a collaborator with Rubens; he was often known as the Velvet Brueghel.)
Drawings: Summer (il. 93); The Beekeepers (il. 121).
Engravings: The Land of Plenty (or Cockaigne) (no il.).
Paintings: The Fall of Icarus (il. 114, 115); The Bird's-Nester (il. 120); The Misanthropist (il. 123); The Parable of the Blind (il. 124, 125, 126, 127, 128, 129); The Magpie on the Gallows (il. 138, 139).

1569 The Brussels aldermen commission a series of paintings representing the digging of the canal between Brussels and Antwerp. Bruegel dies on September 5. He is buried in the church of Notre Dame de la Chapelle in Brussels. His son Jan later commissioned a painting by Rubens to decorate the tomb.
Paintings: (work done in 1568–69) The Cripples (il. 122); The Wedding Feast (il. 130, 131, 132, 133); The Peasant Dance (il. 134, 135, 136, 137).

Bibliography

A select list of books, not including catalogues or critical revues of museum exhibitions.

BOOKS ABOUT THE PERIOD

Huizinga, J. *The Waning of the Middle Ages.* Garden City, N.Y.: Doubleday, Anchor, 1954.

Mander, Karel van. *Het Schilderboek.* Haarlem, 1604.

Trevor-Roper, H. R. *The European Witch Craze of the XVIth and XVIIth Centuries.* London: Pelican Books, 1969.

Yourcenar, Marguerite. *L'Oeuvre au noir.* Paris: Gallimard, 1968.

BOOKS ABOUT THE PAINTINGS OF PETER BRUEGEL THE ELDER

Auner, M. *Pieter Bruegel. Umreisse eines Lebensbildes.*

Bianconi, P. *Tout l'oeuvre peint de Pieter Bruegel.* Introduction by Charles Tolnay. Paris, 1968.

Burchard, L. *Das unbekannte Meisterwerk.* Berlin, 1930.

Claessens, B. and J. Rousseau, *Notre Bruegel.* Antwerp, 1969.

Delevoy, R. I. *Bruegel.* Geneva, 1959.

Denis, V. *Tutta la pittura di Peter Bruegel.* Milan, 1952.

Dvorak, M. *Pieter Bruegel der Altere.* Vienna, 1921, and Munich, 1924.

Faggin, G. *Bruegel.* Verona, 1953.

Fierens. *Pieter Bruegel, sa vie, son oeuvre, son temps.* Brussels, 1949.

Friedlander, M.-J. *Pieter Bruegel.* Berlin, 1921, and Leyden, 1937.

Fryns, M. *Bruegel.* Brussels, 1964.

Genaille, R. *Bruegel l'ancien.* Paris, 1953.

_____. *Pieter Bruegel.* Paris, 1965.

Gluck, G. *Bruegels Gemälde.* Vienna, 1932.

_____. *Das grosse Bruegel Werk.* Vienna, 1953.

Grossman, F. *Bruegel.* New York, Toronto, London, 1966.

Jedlicka, G. *Pieter Bruegel, der Maler in seiner Zeit.* Erlenbach-Zurich, 1938.

Marijnissen, R.-H. and M. Seidel. *Bruegel le Vieux.* Brussels, 1969 and 1977.

Menzel, G.-W. *Pieter Bruegel der Altere.* Leipzig, 1966.

Michel, E. *Bruegel.* Paris, 1931.

Puyvelde, L. van. *La Peinture flamande au siècle de Bosch et de Bruegel.* Paris, 1962.

Stubbe, A. *Bruegel en de Renaissance.* Antwerp, 1950.

Tolnay, Ch. de. *Pierre Bruegel l'Ancien.* Brussels, 1935.

Vanbeselaere, W. *Pieter Bruegel en het Nederlandsche Manierisme.* Tielt, 1944.

Winkler, F. *Die altnierderlaändische Malerei.* Berlin, 1935.

BOOKS ABOUT THE DRAWINGS AND PRINTS OF PETER BRUEGEL THE ELDER

Bastelaer, R. van. *Les Estampes de Peter Bruegel l'Ancien.* Brussels, 1908.

Klein, H. A. *Graphic Worlds of Peter Bruegel the Elder.* New York, 1963.

Lavalleye, J. *Lucas van Leyden, Peter Bruegel l'Ancien. Gravures.* Paris, 1966.

Lebeer, L. *Catalogue raisonné des estampes de Pierre Bruegel l'Ancien.* Brussels, 1969.

Munz, L. *Bruegel, the Drawings.* London, 1961.

Tolnay, Ch. de. *The Drawings of Pieter Bruegel the Elder.* London, 1952.

BOOKS ABOUT PETER BRUEGHEL THE YOUNGER (HELL BRUEGHEL)

Marlier, Georges. *Pieter Brueghel le Jeune.* Brussels, 1969.

BOOKS ABOUT JAN BRUEGHEL (VELVET BRUEGHEL)

Ertz, Klaus. *Jan Breughel.* Catalogue raisonné, Cologne, 1970.

Photograph Credits by Illustration